"*Network Marketing: The Best of the Best* crystallizes what this business is all about." J. G. - Flushing, NY

"*Network Marketing: The Best of the Best* explains Network Marketing in clear, easy-to-understand terms. It is a MUST READ book for anyone who seriously wants to understand this business." J. M. - San Diego, CA

"I have searched for a book that I can use to explain this business to my family and friends—a book that I can use to introduce new people to this business. *Network Marketing: The Best of the Best* is just what I have been searching for ... If only I had had it two years ago when I started in this business—I can only imagine how much farther ahead I would be in my business today."
J. K. - Minneapolis, MN

"*Network Marketing: The Best of the Best* is the best book on Network Marketing that I have ever read!"
R. N. - Anchorage, AK

Network Marketing: The Best of the Best

By
David Stone and Warren Brookings

Sunrise Press, Inc.

NETWORK MARKETING: THE BEST OF THE BEST. Copyright © 1995 Sunrise Press, Inc. All rights reserved. Printed in the United States of America. No part of this book may be used or reproduced in any manner whatsoever without written permission except in the case of brief quotation embodied in critical articles and reviews. For information address Sunrise Press, Inc., P.O. Box 16192, Minneapolis, Minnesota 55416-0192.

Cover designed by Mary E. Schultz

First paperback edition published 1995.

ISBN 0-9648949-0-4 (pbk.)

The information contained in this book has not been approved, reviewed, or endorsed by any Network Marketing servicing corporation. Much of the information presented has been gathered and compiled from many sources within the Network Marketing industry. Sunrise Press, Inc. believes that the information presented here is true and correct.

Sunrise Press, Inc. makes no claims regarding any individual's chances of success should they choose to follow the advice contained in this book.

About the Authors

David Stone is a freelance writer who has served as a business consultant to many startup, small and medium-sized businesses. He has started several successful businesses, one of which sold products into 11 countries. He has served as president of four companies and is currently on the board of directors of two corporations. He holds a bachelor's degree and a master of science degree in electrical engineering.

Warren Brookings is a freelance writer who has been directly involved in the startup of seven companies. He is currently serving on the board of directors of four corporations. He holds a bachelor's degree in economics, a master's degree in business administration and a doctorate in law.

The views expressed in this book are the direct result of many months of independent investigation by the authors into economic conditions, corporate restructuring, and various types of money-making opportunities.

Dedicated to the free spirit that lives within the soul of each one of us.

Contents

Introduction i

1. The Corporate World 1
2. An Alternative to the Corporate Path 7
3. Creating Direct Income 17
4. Creating Residual Income 33
5. Network Marketing 51
6. Selecting a Network Marketing Company 77
7. The Best of the Best in Network Marketing ... 87
8. Profiles of Success 101
9. How to Get Started in This Business 117

Introduction

If money were no object, what would you want to have that money could buy? To some people it's a new car, a new home, a boat, or a vacation in an exotic location. To others, it's the freedom of not having to report to work, day in and day out. Yet, to others, their dream is to change the world, for the better, through the use and influence of their wealth. Some of us wish for all of these things.

Most people's dreams will probably never be realized. Will yours be realized in your current career? Recent statistics indicate that fewer than one in 10 of us will be "financially secure" when we reach age 65, "financially secure" meaning that we are able to continue living the same lifestyle when we stop working. Most of us have a long road to travel to be financially independent when we reach our retirement. What is more disconcerting is that many of us are realizing that the road we are presently on is not the right one. How does one achieve a financially secure retirement or, even better, financial freedom?

Most of the wealthiest individuals in the past have acquired their wealth through real estate. A few very lucky individuals have had winning lottery tickets. Many others have acquired their wealth by spotting a "paradigm shift" and being in position to capitalize upon it.

What is a paradigm shift? It is a fundamental

INTRODUCTION

change in the way people think and the way they behave. Sometimes a paradigm shift is triggered by a new technology. An example of this type of paradigm shift is found in the music industry. Twenty years ago, most of us listened to music on vinyl discs, called records, that we used to play on turntables. Very few people had actually even heard of compact discs or ever imagined that compact discs would replace their huge record collections. Those who saw this happening and positioned themselves properly (in business) made a handsome profit. How many records have you listened to this past week? This paradigm shift has affected all of us.

The computer industry is a great place to look for another example of a paradigm shift. Giant corporations like Control Data, IBM, and Univac manufactured some of the world's most powerful mainframe computers. Mainframe computers were large, expensive, and difficult to manage, requiring entire departments of people. These giant corporations employed hundreds of thousands of people. In the mid 1970s, a couple of entrepreneurs named Steve Wozniak and Steve Jobs, working out of a garage in California, developed a small, inexpensive personal computer. Both had a vision of bringing computer technology to every family. Their efforts blossomed into Apple Computer, Inc. Within just a few years, Control Data, IBM, and Univac felt the impact of personal computers, and so did the thousands of laid-off employees who used to manufacture large

INTRODUCTION

mainframe computers. Prior to 1977, very few people knew anyone who had a personal computer. Today, just about everyone either uses a personal computer or knows someone who does.

This is only the tip of the iceberg as to what actually happened. There were many others involved in, and affected by, this paradigm shift: DEC (Digital Equipment Corporation), Data General, etc. One person who foresaw this paradigm shift and was able to capitalize upon it was Bill Gates, founder of Microsoft and the wealthiest man in the world today. In 10 years, this 37-year-old college dropout borrowed $1,000 and turned it into approximately $8 billion. In July 1995 his net worth was estimated at more than $12 billion, and he reached the top—being ranked the "wealthiest man in the world" by *Forbes*. He realized that the personal computer would need software to run. His company made the operating system software that, among other things, allowed personal computers to read from, and write to, magnetic media called floppy disks.

Today, young families are struggling, even with two incomes per household. People are searching for ways to achieve their dreams of financial freedom. Born from this struggle is a paradigm shift, creating new business opportunities. The traditional corporate "path" is less safe and reliable than it used to be. Corporations like Apple Computer, Boeing, Honeywell, and IBM have laid off tens of thousands of employees in the last few years. Many of these employees were

INTRODUCTION

laid off after serving faithfully and loyally for decades. Because of this shift in the perception of corporate job security in the minds of potential employees, more and more people are looking for ways to augment their income and their financial security through alternative means. Some are starting new businesses or investing in franchised businesses. Some are investing in stocks, mutual funds, treasury notes. Some are taking advantage of opportunities in Network Marketing.

In the course of our investigation into various business opportunities, we discovered what we believe to be a paradigm shift, taking place around the world, involving NETWORK MARKETING. Network Marketing offers an opportunity to achieve financial freedom without the risks associated with many of the other alternatives.

We are creatures of habit. We don't like change. We ignore changes in our economic culture ... but some of us anticipate changes and will profit from them. The purpose of this book is to help people with dreams achieve those dreams. This book focuses on Network Marketing—why Network Marketing is an excellent business opportunity contrasted with many others, how to select a Network Marketing company, one Network Marketing company we found that stands far ahead of the others, and how to get started in this fast-growing business so that you and your family can benefit from this paradigm shift.

Chapter 1.
The Corporate World

Is the Corporate World letting us down?

Think back to when you were growing up. Our parents held to the belief that if we went to a good school and got a good college education, then we were guaranteed a high-paying, secure job for life with a big corporation. We were conditioned from a very early age that we could rely on the Corporate World for a financially secure future. The facts paint a different picture ... a picture that will affect us all!

In today's global economy, companies have to produce more product or provide more services with less overhead in order to stay price competitive. What does this mean?

It means layoffs. Lots of them.

John Naisbitt, in his book *Reinventing the Corporation,* has stated: in the 1980s and 1990s there's no longer the security in corporations that there used to be. The popular press confirms his prophecy years later:

"In a quest for efficiency, companies have been charging billions of dollars off their earnings to lay off hundreds of thousands of workers. The current euphemism is 'reengineering'—a bloodless term for corporate bloodletting on an unprecedented scale. In the year's first quarter (1994), employers announced an average of 3,106 cutbacks per day."[1]

NETWORK MARKETING: THE BEST OF THE BEST

In the May 9, 1994, issue of *Business Week*, the title of a table reads

"JOB DEATH: 25 LARGE DOWNSIZINGS."

Company	Staff cutbacks
IBM	85,000
AT&T	83,500
General Motors	74,000
US Postal Service	55,000
Sears	50,000
Boeing	30,000
NYNEX	22,000
Hughes Aircraft	21,000
GTE	17,000
Martin Marietta	15,000
DuPont	14,800
Eastman Kodak	14,000
Philip Morris	14,000
Procter & Gamble	13,000
Phar Mor	13,000
Bank of America	12,000
Aetna	11,800
GE Aircraft Engines	10,250
McDonnell Douglas	10,200
Bellsouth	10,200
Ford Motor	10,000
Xerox	10,000
Pacific Telesis	10,000
Honeywell	9,000
US West	9,000

THE CORPORATE WORLD

The table shows 25 of the largest announced staff reductions since early 1991.
People's attitudes toward the corporate environment are changing. The popular press is reporting this change with greater and greater frequency. The fact is, it has been happening for quite a long time. In the early 1970s, many of the engineers who were employed in the aerospace industry found themselves out of work due to a drop in the demand for aircraft. They were a relatively segregated segment of the work force. The drop in the demand for jobs with their skills lasted for several years. Many found other professions. Some dropped out of the Corporate World and vowed never to work there again. Those are the ones who started their own businesses. Different from the layoffs in the 1970s, today's layoffs are crossing much broader industry borders, and they are affecting not primarily engineers but everyone. Some believe that, in the long term, this new global competitive economy will strengthen U.S. corporations, but if you work for a company that is going through the process of "downsizing," you may be more concerned about your job and family's financial stability ... and you should be.
"Today's corporation is no longer a secure or stable place. It's an uncertain, turbulent environment where managers often find their compassion and humanity in conflict with the pressures of competition and ambition. Fear is almost palpable in the corridors of the reengineered workplace, where loyalty takes a back

NETWORK MARKETING: THE BEST OF THE BEST

seat to survival and personal advancement."[2]

Do you know anyone who has been laid off recently? Or maybe you have been laid off recently? If so, then you probably would agree that this is an experience that you will never forget. It is truly life changing. Results include anger, doubt, uncertainty, fear ... loss of necessary income.

"Next to the death of a relative or friend, there's nothing more traumatic than losing a job. Corporate cutbacks threaten the security and self-esteem of survivors and victims alike. Layoffs disrupt careers and families. They cause turmoil and shatter the morale inside organizations. And they confirm the public's view that profits always come before people."[3]

In today's global economy, companies have to produce more product or provide more services with less overhead in order to stay price competitive. What does this mean?

It means that each employee needs to do more work for the same pay.

"Burnout" is becoming more common. In many cases, rather than working more efficiently, employees are just expected to work more hours. Less vacation time, more overtime, more stress....

"Annual worktime has increased by 158 hours per year—nearly a whole month—since 1969.... In 1992, the most recent year for which statistics are available, 46% of American workers were worried about losing their jobs, according to a study by Northwestern National Life, an insurance company in Minneapolis.

Forty-five percent said they had to work overtime, and 39% said they felt like quitting."[4]

As a result of losing your job, the real, traumatic effect may be your realization that you were misled by the false sense of security offered by the Corporate World. Ask yourself: Do I want to count on the Corporate World for my financial security? Can I count on the Corporate World for my financial security? The facts say **NO!**

Today, with corporate downsizing and more and more families relying on two incomes just to make ends meet, people are becoming uncomfortable knowing that their families' financial stability can be thrown off balance by events beyond their control. People are searching for business opportunities that give them more control over their financial stability. Most are not looking to quit their jobs and leave the Corporate World "cold turkey"; rather they are looking for a means to supplement their current incomes and eventually eliminate their dependence upon their corporate paychecks. People are starting to take control over their own lives. They do that by going into business for themselves.

---

1. *Business Week*, May 9, 1994, p. 61.
2. Ibid., p. 61.
3. Ibid., p. 69.
4. *American Health*, vol. 13, December 1994, p. 50.

Chapter 2.
An Alternative to the Corporate Path

Going into business for yourself and taking control of your life may be the best answer.

Why is getting into your own business going to let you take control over your life?

1. When you own your own business, you have the potential for becoming financially secure. You are rewarded for your successes. You get a little reward for a small success, and you get a large reward for a large success. Small successes are usually easier to create than large successes; however, with time and a little luck, you learn how to create large successes, and you become more efficient at creating many small successes in a given time period. As you become more successful in your own business, you get rewarded more. Success can refer to many things, but in this chapter, success refers to profitability. If, for example, your business is selling a product or service, a small success might mean a sale that generates, say, $100 profit. A large success might mean $10,000 profit. As time goes on, your definition of a small success might become $10,000, while a large success might become $1,000,000 profit.

2. When you own your own business, the reward from year to year is not limited to a "cost of living" increase or a budget set by someone else. When you are in business for yourself, you have no limit placed on how much more money you can make this year as contrasted with last year. If you are more successful this year than last, then you will make more money this year.
3. When you own your own business, you are the boss. You set your own working hours and the hours of your employees, if you decide to hire any. Generally, you work when the customers and suppliers are also working so that you can interact with them as necessary. But if you want time off, no one will hassle you. Also, you can work during "off hours" to catch up or get ahead. In addition, you take vacations when you want to, not when someone else gives you permission or, worse, tells you when you're going to.

So if going into business for yourself is so wonderful, why doesn't everyone do it?

Because it's a lot of hard work, and even hard work does not guarantee success. In fact, most new businesses fail, and the people who started them usually have to pick up the pieces and try again. One of the best things to do if you're considering starting your own business is to learn from those who have been successful. The information is readily accessible, because several very successful people have written books or created audiotapes about their rules for success.

Some guidelines for success taken from *How to Be Rich* by J. Paul Getty are:

1. Be in business for yourself. "Almost without exception, there is only one way to make a great deal of money in the business world—and that is in one's own business."

    How many corporations do you know of that produce millionaire employees on a regular basis? As a general rule, the founders and some of the original investors in a corporation are the only ones who have a chance at making over a million dollars' income from the business. The employees typically just get their hourly pay or salary regardless of their performance. If there is a bonus or profit sharing, it usually is a small percentage of the actual profit gained by the business.

2. Market a product or service that is in great demand. "A businessman must constantly seek new horizons and untapped or under-exploited markets.... Today's shrewd businessman looks to foreign markets."

    Identifying a product or service that is in great demand that one could sell is very difficult. Why? Because most products or services that are in great demand are already being sold to the market. You may identify a need that is in great enough demand to base your business upon. It might be a specialized need for a small, or niche, market.

Identifying a need is one of the more time-consuming aspects of starting a new business. Uncertainty breeds doubt, which transforms into fear and eventually leads to a self-fulfilling prophecy (of failure). You must educate yourself about the market (both domestic and foreign), the need, and the competition in order to increase your odds of success.

3. Guarantee that product or service. "Nothing builds confidence and volume faster or better than a reputation for standing behind one's work or products. Guarantees should always be honored."

This is a matter of integrity and building trust with your prospective customers. You must believe in what you are providing and be ready to guarantee it. The customer's satisfaction comes first. This builds your reputation as a good company to do business with in the marketplace.

4. Give better service than the competition. "The businessman should never lose sight of the central aim of all business—to produce more and better goods or provide more and better services to more people at lower cost."

It is cheaper to buy a loaf of bread "by the loaf" than it is to buy it "by the slice." This is usually the case with most items: the larger the quantity, the cheaper the price. This is called "economy of scale." As you make more of an item, you can spread out, or amortize, your initial costs (e.g., development, tooling, etc.) over more

AN ALTERNATIVE TO THE CORPORATE PATH

products, which lowers the cost of each item. As your business grows, you may be able to produce the product or provide the service at a lower cost.

Some guidelines for choosing the ideal business come from an audiotape titled *A Financial Planner's Viewpoint*. In this tape, John Sestina, a certified financial planner and chartered financial consultant who has reviewed over a thousand business plans, describes the ideal business as follows:

1. It has a huge market. It sells to the world rather than any single neighborhood or city or locality.
2. It has a product with an inelastic, or unchanging, demand. You don't want your market demand confined, and you don't want a "widget" where the big guys can come along and fiddle with your patent, improve on your product, and force you out of the market.
3. It has low labor requirements: the fewer people needed, the better.
4. It sells a product which fits a continuing human or animal need.
5. It has low overhead costs. It can be run out of your home or apartment. You don't want to have leases, personal loan guarantees, insurance to protect yourself for not paying the lease, and so on.
6. It produces a product which is difficult for the competition to copy or reproduce.
7. It does not require huge cash expenditures.

NETWORK MARKETING: THE BEST OF THE BEST

8. It is a cash business: no accounts receivable. Customers pay you for the product when they receive it.
9. It is relatively free from all kinds of government and industry regulations.
10. It is portable. It can be anywhere in the world, anytime. Simple presentation, simple business.

Taking control of your financial security by starting your own business involves answering many difficult questions: Who is my market? What does this market need? What product or service will my company provide to satisfy this need? How much money will I need to start this business? Who are the competition? Do I have a competitive advantage? In order to start answering these questions, you need to gain some marketing knowledge that will help you evaluate your options.

Some really valuable marketing knowledge can be found in books by Al Ries and Jack Trout. They wrote *Marketing Warfare* and *The 22 Immutable Laws of Marketing,* among others. Marketing is the positioning of your company's products or services in the mind of the potential consumer. When you are in your own business, you need to understand marketing, because your business is going to be selling either a product or a service, and your chances for success are greatly improved if you have done your marketing correctly. Marketing knowledge will guide your business when you come to "a fork in the road" and are not sure what direction to take. Your business must be market driven.

Income
The primary goal in having your own business is to make money—i.e., you don't go into business to lose money. In fact, if your business does not make money eventually, you will go out of business. You want your business to generate enough money so that you can become financially secure.

Income can be put into two categories: (1) direct income—which is the money that you earn as a direct result of your time and immediate efforts (e.g., your paycheck); and (2) residual income—which is the money that comes independently of your immediate direct efforts (e.g., dividends from stocks that you own). Your income is the sum of these two types of income.

How income is spent
First, you need money to live on. This is the "basic necessities" money that puts a roof over your head, food on your table, and clothes on your back. It is also the "luxury" money that you spend on a vacation, dining out, or going to the theater.... It is the money that you use on a daily basis for living.

Second, you need money to put away, or invest, that will generate more money for you. It's money that will be working for you to create future residual income.

Retirement

People typically work very hard and make sacrifices so that they can put away a little each month to create residual income for their retirement. With a retirement account, you put something into it each month, even though you really would like to have more of it to spend now, so that by the time you retire you'll have a substantial amount accumulated. In order to be financially secure after you retire, you need to make sure that enough residual income will be flowing to you by the time you plan to retire so that you can maintain your desired lifestyle.

The "nest egg" dilemma

Many retired individuals take their "retirement nest egg" and work out a conservative reverse amortization payout over many years. A reverse amortization payout is like the opposite of a home mortgage—you use a mathematical calculation to determine the monthly amount paid to you for a specific number of payments based on an assumed interest rate. At the end of the specific number of payments (e.g., one payment per month for 20 years would be 240 payments), all of the original principal is paid out, and the nest egg is gone.

The problem with a reverse amortization payout is that none of us knows exactly how long we will live. We don't want to run out of money to live on and thus be a burden on our families or on society. Since we don't know how many reverse amortization payments to make, we cannot determine the monthly payment amount. We also don't know the interest rate (actually, the rate of return on our investments). One way to get around these unknowns is to create enough residual income to cover retirement living expense needs and avoid "touching" the principal or "nest egg." We can give it to our children and grandchildren or to charity in our will.

Planning for your retirement is important, but "it's hard to remember that you are trying to drain the swamp when the alligators are snapping their jaws in your face." If you are not making enough direct income and are struggling to cover your current living expenses, it's hard to set aside money for your retirement years. Many people are looking at starting their own business to increase their income because they just can't live the lifestyle that they want on what they make from their current job, and the chances of landing a higher paying job are "slim to none."

Creating income through your own business

Taking control of your financial security by starting your own business is a big change from working for someone else. Change causes anxiety in many people. Your new business will need to generate enough direct income for you to live on and, it is to be hoped, much more.

When you are trying to decide what your new business will do to generate income for you, it's a good idea to have a method to help you evaluate business opportunities. Practice applying your method of evaluating business opportunities by looking at various types of businesses before you make the commitment to start your own. In the next chapter we will review several types of businesses and discuss the advantages and disadvantages associated with each of them.

Chapter 3.
Creating Direct Income

When you go into business for yourself, one of the first decisions that you are faced with is selecting the type of business to start. There are many types of businesses that you can start. In evaluating business opportunities, it is useful to review a few conventional types of businesses. Understand generally what they do and how they make money. Also, review some of the advantages and disadvantages associated with each.

This review is not intended to replace the thorough investigation that you should do before starting your own business. Instead, it is intended to illustrate different options that you are faced with when starting your own business.

There are several options to choose from when starting your own business, and depending on your background, some of them may be more appealing than others. We review several types of businesses in this chapter. Read about the types of businesses that interest you, and feel free to skip over the ones that don't. Try to get a feel for how to evaluate different types of businesses.

Conventional types of businesses
A consulting practice

If you have substantial training and credentials, or many years of experience, in a specific area, then you may want to start a consulting practice. Most consulting practices start out as one-person businesses. Some consulting practices grow into consulting firms with several employees, each of whom has very specialized skills or knowledge. Many consulting practices are home-based businesses. Consulting firms are usually not home based but rather are located in professional office buildings. In a consulting practice, you call on potential clients or companies that could benefit from the specific expertise that you have, and you let them know that your expertise is for sale.

As a consultant, you need to write a lot of proposals. Potential clients ask for proposals. In them, you estimate the cost (to the clients) and the time frame required to accomplish the clients' goals. You interact with clients as an independent expert who is there to help them with their specific needs. When you get the project, you set your own hours so that you accomplish the goals within the time frame that you and your client have agreed upon. You may hire employees, or subcontract to other consultants, in order to complete the project on time. Much of your new business may come from word-of-mouth advertising, when a prospective client gets your firm's name from someone who has been one of your clients or from someone who heard about you from one of

CREATING DIRECT INCOME

your past clients. As your consulting practice grows, you may hire a support staff and open offices in several locations. You may advertise the services that your firm offers through trade journals, conferences, trade shows, etc.—whatever will reach your audience of potential clients. In a consulting practice, you are selling expertise.

What are the "pros and cons" in a consulting practice business?

Advantages of a consulting practice business:
1. Low startup capital required. It does not require a huge cash expenditure to start.
2. Low overhead cost—home-based business.
3. No employees required (except you yourself).
4. You can do it anywhere.

Disadvantages of a consulting practice business:
1. There is usually a limited or small market for your skills.
2. The demand for your services depends upon several factors beyond your control, such as the economy.
3. The need is not a continuing need. When a project is completed, you are done and must go find another project to work on.
4. You have "accounts receivable" to collect from clients, and not all clients pay you, even after you have finished the project to their satisfaction.
5. In order to stay in the business, you need to

maintain a high level of expertise in your field or industry. This may require ongoing education, educating your employees, and even hiring or recruiting experts to join your firm.

The amount of competition from other consultants will depend on your specific skill level and skill set. This consulting practice example illustrates an approach to evaluating business opportunities. Understand the nature of the business, and create a list of the pros and cons using the criteria from the previous chapter of this book (Chapter 2).

A service provider business
If you don't have the background to be a consultant, you can still find many service-related business opportunities. Remember when you were growing up. Did you, or one of your friends, ever make money by cutting the neighbors' grass or baby-sitting? You or your friends were making money by providing a service. Today, there are many companies that are service providers. They are in such businesses as grass cutting, pool cleaning, landscaping, roofing, deck building, remodeling, daycare, house cleaning, carpet and upholstery cleaning.... The list goes on and on. In a service provider business, you are selling a service or group of services that people need. Your business may provide the service on an "ongoing," or contract basis, or on a one-time basis. You make money by selling and providing the service. Your goal is to

CREATING DIRECT INCOME

satisfy the customer's need and make money doing so. You may do the work yourself, or you may hire employees or subcontract all, or some, of the work to other service providers. As your business grows, you hire employees or subcontract to others so that the service can be provided in a timely fashion.

An example, for evaluation purposes, might be a lawn care business. In this business, you cut grass, primarily. You charge a "per time" fee for providing this service (i.e., each time that you cut the grass, you charge a set amount). You might canvass neighborhoods, leaving on doors fliers that offer free estimates for your services, or you might place a few advertisements in local newspapers or the phone book. You give out estimates to potential customers, and some of them become customers. Typically, you invoice customers once a month. As your business grows, you purchase more lawn mowers and a trailer and truck to haul them, and you hire more employees to operate this equipment. Your business may expand and offer additional services such as spring and fall raking, fertilization and weed control, and so on. You may reach a point as the business grows where, in order to add one more customer, you need to buy more equipment. You make money in this business when you utilize your equipment and employees efficiently, estimate your job costs correctly (and base your fees on your cost plus a profit), and have a steady base of paying customers.

NETWORK MARKETING: THE BEST OF THE BEST

What are the "pros and cons" in a lawn care business?

Advantages of a lawn care business:
1. It has a huge market. Almost every home in America has a lawn.
2. It has a growing market. New homes are being built every year.
3. In the beginning, the labor requirements are low. You can start this business yourself.
4. It fills a continuing need (albeit seasonal). Grass grows and needs to be cut.
5. In the beginning, it has low overhead cost. It can be based out of your home.
6. You can do it just about anywhere there are lawns.

Disadvantages of a lawn care business:
1. As the business grows, so does the number of employees that you need: the labor requirements grow. You'll have to pay for workman's compensation insurance, state and federal unemployment, employer's matching social security, medicare, and any benefits that you offer your employees.
2. As the business grows, so does the overhead. You quickly outgrow a home or apartment and need a place to store and maintain the equipment. Rent, insurance, utilities, etc., are part of your overhead.
3. It's easy for competing businesses to emerge: a teenager with a lawn mower can start competing

CREATING DIRECT INCOME

against you tomorrow.
4. As the business grows, more equipment is needed. Trucks, trailers, industrial lawn mowers, etc., are expensive. The cash expenditures easily reach five- and six-digit numbers.
5. The business is seasonal. In the spring and early summer, cash is "tight." You pay someone to "ready" all of your equipment for the season, you provide a month of services to your customers, you pay your employees, you buy the gas to operate the equipment, then you invoice your customers and hope they'll pay you in a reasonable period of time. In this business you typically have accounts receivable. Not all of them will be collected.
6. If your business expands into fertilizing and weed control chemicals, you will have to be aware of, and follow, government regulations.

Another type of service provider business might offer automated, or non-labor-intensive, types of services. These services include phone voicemail service, digital phone number paging service, cellular telephone service, or other automated services that do not rely on people as much as equipment. These businesses set up and maintain the equipment that their clients utilize. They make their money through the efficient utilization of this equipment. The customers are charged a monthly fee based upon an assumed usage of the equipment. When customers go over the assumed monthly usage amount, they are charged a per-usage or per-time fee. This fee is sometimes called a metered fee, because the more the customer uses, the more the customer is billed. This type of business grows by signing up more service subscribers. When the equipment is fully utilized, then the business either buys more equipment and adds it to its existing system or modernizes its equipment by replacing the old equipment with new equipment. Your goal in this type of business is to efficiently utilize the equipment so that you can offer the service at a competitive price to the customer and make money doing so.

The pros and cons in this type of service provider business will differ from the lawn care business in that the labor requirements will be lower as the business expands, the cost of entry into this business will be much greater, the customer need will be more consistent and less seasonal, etc.

A manufacturing business

If you have a knack for logistics and are motivated by producing physical product, then a manufacturing business may be for you. In a manufacturing business, you apply a process to raw material and create a "finished product" or "finished goods" by adding value to it. The added value may be in the form of a process such as heating, dehydrating, curing, polishing, or even packaging. It could also be in the form of assembling, testing, or inspecting. The value-added process could be in just about any form ranging from

CREATING DIRECT INCOME

simply re-packaging (e.g., from a 50-pound bag into 50 one-pound bags) to as complex as purchasing the raw materials and executing the many steps required to make an automobile. In manufacturing, you set up your firm to be very efficient at specific value-adding tasks. You sell the manufacturing services to companies that need to have the same process applied to their products. Because your manufacturing business is "optimized" for this specific process, you can add a markup for profit to your cost and still manufacture at a lower cost to potential clients than if they manufactured the goods themselves.

In a manufacturing business you might be producing products or goods for other businesses or for your own business. You might not even offer your manufacturing capabilities to any other businesses. Your business could be set up just to produce the goods or products that your business sells. Many manufacturing businesses start by developing a product in their own research lab, which could be home based such as in a basement or garage, and contract the manufacturing to an "outside" firm. When their product sales volume reaches a high-enough point, it becomes more cost effective to manufacture the product "in-house." When they set up their manufacturing "in-house," or inside of their own business, they get the added benefit of being able to refine the process or improve upon it. They can then patent the new process or keep it a trade secret. Other reasons that companies manufacture their own product "in-house": to maintain quality control, to protect their trade secrets and make it more difficult for others to compete with them, and to reduce their reliance upon outside sources so that they have more control over the availability of their product.

In a manufacturing business you are selling the value-adding process that your firm provides. You need to keep your process as efficient as possible. As the volume of business changes, your process may need to be adjusted to maintain its efficiency. This adjustment may be in the form of the steps utilized in the process or in higher capacity equipment or even in the size of the building that your business occupies.

What are the "pros and cons" in a manufacturing business?

Advantages of a manufacturing business:
1. It can have a huge market, but this depends upon the business.
2. It may manufacture a product that has an unchanging demand, but this also depends upon the business.
3. It may have low labor requirements if the process of adding value is automated.
4. The manufactured product may fill a continuing human or animal need.

CREATING DIRECT INCOME

Disadvantages of a manufacturing business:
1. It may have a very limited market, but this depends upon the business.
2. New methods of production and technological "breakthroughs" could greatly affect the demand for what your business provides (e.g., manufacturers of mechanical watch movements were greatly affected by the invention of the quartz watch).
3. It may have significant labor requirements, but this also depends upon the business. You'll have to pay for workman's compensation insurance, state and federal unemployment, employer's matching social security, medicare, and any benefits that you offer your employees.
4. Usually there is a high overhead associated with a manufacturing business. Rent for manufacturing space, equipment maintenance costs, insurance, utilities, etc., are part of your overhead. All of your equipment is a liability until you are producing because you have to pay for the space to store it, and the insurance to protect it, whether it is being used or not.
5. It's easy for competing businesses to emerge whenever technologies change. They purchase the same equipment that you purchase. They educate themselves about the new technology the same way that you do. The major deterrent is the high cost of entry into the business.

6. The business may require huge cash expenditures for equipment and raw materials. Generally, a manufacturing business requires a building or place to add value. It requires a large initial cash expenditure to purchase equipment and raw materials.
7. It is usually not a cash business. In fact, most manufacturers purchase the raw materials, pay for the labor and overhead, and ship the product at least a month before they get paid. In order to do this, they establish a credit line at their bank and borrow against it, paying interest to the bank for the use of the money. In some cases, they are unable to collect the money owed to them through no fault of their own.
8. In some areas of manufacturing, there are many government regulations that must be followed. For example, in painting and finishing the government has regulations regarding the amount of volatile organic compounds (VOCs) or solvents that you can release into the atmosphere.
9. Manufacturing is not very portable, especially when you have large, heavy pieces of specialized equipment. It does make sense to locate your business close to either your suppliers or your customers to reduce shipping costs.

A franchise business
In a franchise business you are buying someone else's experience and "equation for success." There

CREATING DIRECT INCOME

are thousands of decisions to make when starting up a new business: what equipment to purchase, how to set it up, how to pick a location, whom to use as suppliers, etc. When you purchase a franchise business, the franchising firm sells you its "equation for success," and then it's up to you to put in the effort and money to follow the guidance. The cost usually includes a fee to the franchising firm to "buy the guidance," the cost of the equipment and inventory, business office rental costs, and utility set-up costs (phones, electric, gas, etc.). When you're all set up and operating, most franchise agreements require you to pay a percentage of your gross revenues to the franchiser.

Why would anyone pay, on an ongoing basis, for this information?

Statistics show that most new businesses fail. In fact, according to the Small Business Administration more than 65% of all new businesses fail within five years. Franchised businesses have a much greater success rate. It is estimated that about 33% of franchised businesses fail, 33% break even, and 33% are profitable. When someone figures out a good way to make money with a business and "packages" the knowledge so that anyone can use it, he or she can share in the profits that other people make by franchising.

Examples of franchise businesses in the food market include McDonald's, Burger King, Wendy's, Perkins

NETWORK MARKETING: THE BEST OF THE BEST

Family Restaurant, Subway, and Domino's Pizza, just to mention a few. Other franchised businesses include drug stores, printing, dry cleaning, auto brakes and mufflers, recycled athletic equipment, ... and on and on.

What are the "pros and cons" of purchasing a franchise business?

Advantages of a franchise business:
1. It can have a huge market, depending on the product, but generally a franchise business serves a local or "neighborhood" market. To reach larger markets, you have to open up "shop" in several locations.
2. It can have a product with an inelastic, or unchanging, demand such as fast food. Again it depends upon which franchise business you choose.
3. The product or service could fit a continuing human need such as cutting hair or repairing auto mufflers.
4. It could be a cash business. Again this depends upon what franchise business you choose.
5. You can do it just about anywhere (providing your customers are there and the franchise firm agrees to it).

Disadvantages of a franchise business:
1. Most sell to a single neighborhood or city or locality rather than the world.
2. Most have significant labor requirements.

CREATING DIRECT INCOME

3. Most have high overhead costs. You have leases, personal loan guarantees, insurance to protect yourself for not paying the lease, and so on.
4. Competition can be fierce. In addition to competition from other businesses and other franchise firms, some franchising firms oversell their "equation for success." How would you like to pay thousands or tens of thousands of dollars for a franchise and after years of hard work have your franchising firm set up someone in a shop across the street from you doing the same thing that you're doing? This is a bit of an exaggeration, but imagine if the firm set someone up three blocks from you and "saturated" the area around you because you were doing such a good business.
5. It requires huge cash expenditures. First you pay the franchise firm, then you purchase equipment, rent office space, etc. It takes time to be profitable. You have to cover the overhead until then. Franchise businesses can cost from the tens of thousands to the millions of dollars just to get started.

There are basic industries such as mining, manufacturing, and transportation. A business can be started in any area where there is a need. It is up to the individual to find the need and create a business that profits from addressing the need. We have looked at only a few examples in this chapter. We have discussed the trade-offs associated with some of these choices. Try to identify the pros and cons when you evaluate your business ideas. Become an expert in the field that your business will be in before you start your own business. Go into much greater detail than we have here before making decisions. The decisions that you make now will have significant impact on your chance of success later.

There are a number of reasons why you would want to get into business for yourself. Your reasons might be to be rewarded for your own efforts and make more money; to enable you to control your own time; to improve your lifestyle; to build your character; etc. The efforts you put into your business, with a little luck, will generate an income stream for you. This income is the by-product of your hard work—lots of hours of work. What happens when you stop working? This income stops—unless you've put into place the people, policies, and procedures necessary to keep your business running profitably. If you want income when you are not working, then you need to create RESIDUAL INCOME. It's your ticket to financial freedom.

Chapter 4.
Creating Residual Income

Residual income is frequently the goal of investors who want a steady income stream from their investments in the form of dividends, interest, rent, royalties, etc. It is something that we all hope to build from our work so that when we retire, we will continue to receive an income stream to live on even though we are no longer actively working. Residual income is something we all want.

Residual income from investments, such as stocks and bonds, real estate holdings, or municipal bonds, requires substantial amounts of cash before you, as an investor, can start to realize any appreciable residual income return from your investments. For example, if you invested your savings in a bank that is paying 4% interest, you would need $250,000 in your bank account just to receive $10,000 per year interest from that account! And to top that off, you would have to pay income tax on that $10,000—both federal and state taxes! *Note*: There are some states that do not have a state income tax, but most states do.

This type of residual income might appeal to someone who has worked his entire life and wants to be absolutely safe and secure with his money, but it is certainly not for someone who is just starting out in the business world with little or no working cash.

Note: Putting your money into the bank is not 100% safe, since the Federal Deposit Insurance Corporation, or FDIC, (or the Federal Savings and Loan Insurance Corporation, or FSLIC) which insures the money that you deposit into a savings account limits its liability to $100,000. In other words, $150,000 of the $250,000 in your savings account would be lost if your bank should fail (as some did in the late 1980s and early 1990s).

Besides, after inflation is taken into consideration, that 4% interest rate per year may actually be losing money, since inflation is probably higher than 4%. See **Figure 1**, Percent change from year to year in the consumer price index. Note that the change from year to year has remained greater than zero, which means that we have had inflation for more than 30 years. Inflation is where almost everything costs more each year than the previous year. Inflation cannot be ignored when you are building residual income. This figure shows that for 19 of the past 34 years the prices of energy, food, shelter, apparel and upkeep, transportation, medical care, fuel oil, electricity, utility (piped) gas, telephone services, and all commodities have increased from the prior year by more than 4%.

Have you ever heard your parents or grandparents say that they used to pay 29¢ for a gallon of gas or

CREATING RESIDUAL INCOME

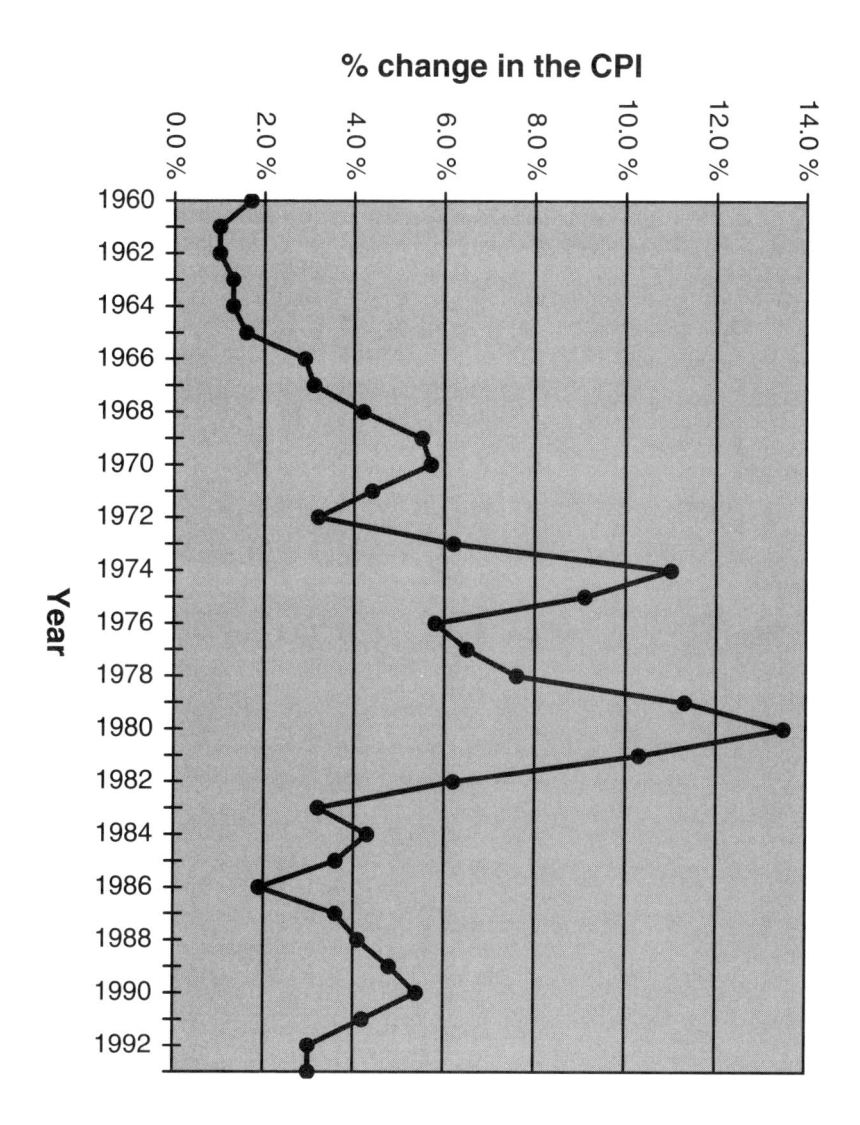

Figure 1. Percent change from year to year in the consumer price index (CPI).

NETWORK MARKETING: THE BEST OF THE BEST

The data from which Figure 1. is created:

Year	% change in consumer price index *	Year	% change in consumer price index *
1960	1.7	1977	6.5
1961	1.0	1978	7.6
1962	1.0	1979	11.3
1963	1.3	1980	13.5
1964	1.3	1981	10.3
1965	1.6	1982	6.2
1966	2.9	1983	3.2
1967	3.1	1984	4.3
1968	4.2	1985	3.6
1969	5.5	1986	1.9
1970	5.7	1987	3.6
1971	4.4	1988	4.1
1972	3.2	1989	4.8
1973	6.2	1990	5.4
1974	11.0	1991	4.2
1975	9.1	1992	3.0
1976	5.8	1993	3.0

* Percent change in the consumer price index from the immediate prior year.

NOTE: This includes energy, food, shelter, apparel and upkeep, transportation, medical care, fuel oil, electricity, utility (piped) gas, telephone services, and all commodities.

Source: Bureau of Labor Statistics, *Monthly Review and Handbook of Labor Statistic,* Periodic.

CREATING RESIDUAL INCOME

$2,000 for a new car ... or, in general, that they paid some ridiculously low price for something? What you are actually hearing is how time and inflation reduce the value of a dollar. **Figure 2**, The value of a dollar vs. time and inflation, shows how the purchasing power of the dollar is reduced by inflation. The previous figure shows how much inflation can change from year to year. This figure shows you just how significant an impact on the value of a dollar a slight increase in inflation can have. Notice that when there is no inflation, which has not happened in over 30 years, that a dollar today will still be worth a dollar, in terms of purchasing power, in 20 years. When inflation is at 4% per year, today's dollar will be worth only 46¢ in 20 years. If inflation is at 10% per year, today's dollar will be worth only about 15¢ in 20 years. There are entire chapters in business school textbooks devoted to the subject of "the time-value of money." When it comes to creating residual income, inflation must be included in your calculations and planning.

In this chapter, we will be discussing the principles of residual income as they relate to the most common investments people make and the pros and cons of pursuing such investments in order to achieve a residual income stream. One thing to keep in mind as you read is that your "return on investment" must take into account "price appreciation" in addition to the steady flow of residual income that it generates for

NETWORK MARKETING: THE BEST OF THE BEST

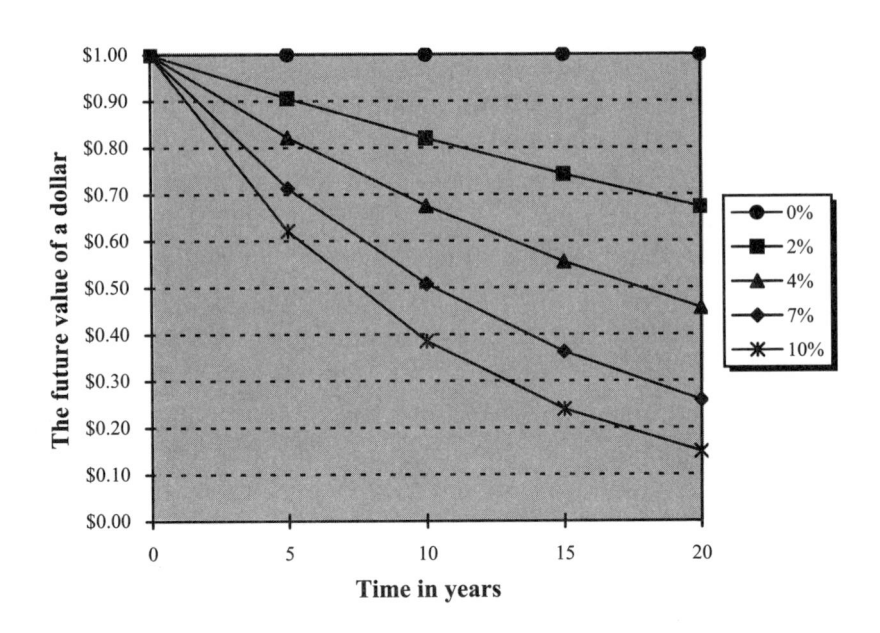

The future value of a dollar:

	0	5	10	15	20
The annual inflation rate					
0%	$1.00	$1.00	$1.00	$1.00	$1.00
2%	$1.00	$0.91	$0.82	$0.74	$0.67
4%	$1.00	$0.82	$0.68	$0.56	$0.46
7%	$1.00	$0.71	$0.51	$0.36	$0.26
10%	$1.00	$0.62	$0.39	$0.24	$0.15

Figure 2. The value of a dollar vs. time and inflation.

CREATING RESIDUAL INCOME

you. Return on investment (ROI) is a measure of how well your money is working for you. A 10% ROI means that your investment grows by 10% per year. That growth includes any price appreciation, which is the increase in the value of the original investment, and any payments made to you during the year. Inflation is subtracted from the ROI to determine your net gain (or loss). *Note*: The Internal Revenue Service does not take into account the inflation rate when determining your federal tax liability.

Purchasing municipal bonds

Municipal bonds are similar to bank savings accounts in that they are both extremely secure investments that are safe, dependable, and relatively risk free. Both municipal bonds and bank savings accounts are used primarily in retirement situations where the owners want a steady residual income but as little risk as possible. They offer very little, if any, chance of price appreciation, which means that your investment will be worth the same number of dollars in 10 years as it is today. Actually, in real dollar value, your investment will be worth less than it is worth today because, as inflation continues its steady upward trend, the buying power of the dollar decreases. Because of inflation, your dollars will not be able to buy as much in the future as they can buy for you now. Furthermore, the amount of cash needed in your bank savings accounts or municipal bonds will be so large, in order to earn enough residual income to supply you with a livable yearly income, that it is well beyond the range of the vast majority of people. A municipal bond, similar to a bank savings account, should be viewed as a place to temporarily park excess cash rather than as a source of income due to its low interest rates, high cash requirements, and lack of growth potential.

Note: In the previous paragraph we were referring to General Obligation bonds, which are backed fully by the government. There is much to know about municipal bonds before purchasing them. You should know the payment source and tax status. There are many types of municipal bonds. Here are just a few examples:

General obligation (GO) bonds usually issued for necessary public works types of projects. The government stands behind them and will use its authority to impose taxes if necessary to ensure that the bonds (principal) and interest are paid.

Revenue bonds issued for specific projects; the revenues generated from these projects will pay the principal and interest. These specific projects might include airports, water systems, transit systems, and sports stadiums. As an investor in bonds you need to check out the viability of the project before you invest in it. You do not want to invest in the bond if you have doubts about the project being able to generate the revenues to pay off the debt (both principal and interest).

The tax status also is used to describe various types of bonds. All municipal bonds issued prior to August 8, 1986, were exempt from federal tax. Since then, the tax status of municipal bonds varies depending upon the purpose for which the bond was issued.

Essential purpose bonds usually GO bonds issued to build roadways, tunnels, bridges, hospitals, schools, some power plants and water treatment systems, etc. Interest income from these bonds is still exempt from federal income tax.

Nonessential purpose bonds generally issued to raise capital for student loans, housing projects, industrial development projects, etc. If you are subject to the alternative minimum tax, income from some of these bonds may not be exempt from federal income tax.

Investing in real estate

Huge fortunes have been made in the real estate market, but most of those fortunes were made when regulatory laws were less stringent than they are today, when tax laws were more favorable to real estate developers, and when land was cheaper and easier to come by. Residual income from real estate investments, however, did not usually come until the investor had built up his equity in real estate holdings, so that by the time residual income started to roll in, mortgages, legal fees, debt obligations, etc., were pretty well reduced to a minimum so that the investor could reap the benefits of his labors. As with residual income from bank savings accounts or municipal bonds, however, the amount of equity needed in real estate to obtain enough rental payments per month to live on is substantial when you consider all the hidden, and not so hidden, costs. These costs include mortgage payments, taxes, legal and accounting fees, broker fees, title insurance, property insurance, general property maintenance, etc.

In order to really succeed in real estate so that you can generate a large enough income to live on, you must have a lot of time and patience, you must have a broad knowledge of real estate market conditions and laws, and you must be willing to constantly supervise your properties or hire someone else to do so.

Residual income from real estate is definitely a possibility that lures many individuals to follow this dream, but like so many other sources of residual income, it does not come until you have built a substantial net worth, and then this question arises: Shall I keep my property and live on the income being paid to me by my tenants (and keep dealing with the headaches), or shall I sell the whole thing and put my money into a bank savings account paying 4% interest?

CREATING RESIDUAL INCOME

Investing in the stock market

Residual income comes in the form of stock dividends when investing in the stock market. Dividends, however, are not always stable and can just as easily be decreased by the company as increased. If you plan to live on the dividends that are being paid by certain stocks, you must be prepared to set aside large amounts of cash to buy these stocks. You must also be aware that stock prices are often extremely volatile, so that if you have a squeamish stomach and don't sleep well after seeing your stocks drop in value the day before, then the stock market is probably not for you. It is generally true that the greater the degree of risk involved in an investment, the greater the possibility of a larger-than-normal return. The flip side to this axiom is that the greater the risk, the more likely you are to lose a sizable portion of your investment. If you are looking for stability in dividend yields, then you are looking at stocks that are generally more stable than other stocks, but your chances of making money from price appreciation is greatly reduced. So again the question arises: Should you keep your money in the stock market or should you just put it into a bank savings account or municipal bonds where yields are low but continuity of residual income is practically guaranteed at these low rates for as long as you own these investments?

Investing in mutual funds

(based upon portfolios of high-growth stocks, government/treasury notes, international stocks, and bonds)

Mutual funds are where individuals "pool" their money into a fund that has substantial purchasing power. Most mutual funds specialize in the types of investments that they make. A high-growth fund will specialize in investing in high-growth stocks. A government/treasury fund most likely will specialize in investing in government or treasury notes. Similarly, an international mutual fund will specialize in investing in international markets. There are many types of mutual funds. As an investor, you need to understand what they invest in and how they make or lose money. Some of the more successful investors know when it is time to move their investments from one type of mutual fund to another (and they actually do move their money between the various types of funds several times a year).

All together, the investments of the fund make up the fund's portfolio. The fund purchases a variety of stocks, notes, or bonds (depending on the type of fund) with the hope that it will gain more than it will lose from these investments. The risk is distributed across several purchases. Some investment analysts believe that mutual funds that purchase stocks actually have a significant impact on the prices of those stocks. They believe that if a fund purchases a stock, then

CREATING RESIDUAL INCOME

that stock price will go up because other potential investors may say, "The experts who manage the fund must know something that the rest of the world is unaware of ... so we should buy this stock." Other potential investors will see the price going up and decide to invest in the company's stock themselves, thus increasing the demand for that stock. The greater the demand for a stock, the higher the stock's selling price.

Mutual funds are run by professionals who supposedly have studied the markets and are more adept at making wise investment decisions than the individual investor. While this may be true to some degree, the problem still remains that residual income from any one of these various types of mutual fund portfolios is dependent upon how much money (cash) you as the investor have to invest in order to receive dividends that support you throughout your life.

High-growth stocks, for example, are generally very volatile, pay very low dividends, and generally are bought for the purpose of price appreciation rather than residual income.

Government treasury note mutual funds are generally very safe, experience very little volatility, and generally pay average to better-than-average interest yields. However, there is little prospect of price appreciation, and the amounts of money needed to receive a sizable income are beyond the means of most individuals.

International mutual stock funds are very risky due to a number of factors including currency devaluation, foreign accounting differentials, lack of accurate or timely news reporting, illiquidity of the stock, and lack of price quote information. Very few pay dividends of any size. These types of funds are definitely not for the person who plans to spend the rest of his life living on residual income.

Bond fund portfolios are generally thought by most people to be the safest type of investment, but as interest rates swing, so also do the prices of the funds. For example, if you bought a bond at 7% interest that would come due in five years and the interest rate dropped below 7%, you could find a buyer to pay more for the bond than what you had originally paid. On the other hand, if the interest rate jumped up to 10%, you would have to discount the original price that you paid in order to sell the bond. Mutual funds based upon bonds are just as susceptible as individual bonds to changes in interest rates.

"Junk bonds," bonds that are rated low in terms of their ability to pay the principal and interest, usually pay higher interest than more secure bonds. They are issued and backed by corporations. Junk bond funds pay substantially higher rates of return than safer, more secure bond funds, but due to this increased risk factor they are also more volatile, and the amount of interest earned may be offset by a decrease in the price of the bond fund.

CREATING RESIDUAL INCOME

In all of the above-mentioned types of mutual fund portfolios, you have the one advantage of not putting all of your eggs into one basket. If a junk bond fails, or a stock suddenly becomes worthless (i.e., the issuer goes broke), you are protected by the other stocks or bonds represented in that portfolio. The same reasoning holds true here, however, as it did with the stock market—if you want residual income from these investments, you have already had to make your money, and your goal now is to preserve it and live off its income.

Growing your business so that it runs without you

This type of situation is the dream of all entrepreneurs, i.e., to build up their business to such a degree of proficiency and productivity that the company can run by itself, with or without the leadership of the owner. While this dream does occur and has created many happy owners with residual incomes to last them for the rest of their lives, it is rare due to the many pitfalls that can prevent this dream from ever occurring.

The biggest problem, and one often overlooked by the founder, is that he or she "IS" the business. The founder has developed and retained all of the relationships between the business and the customers; is the one who attends all of the trade shows and knows where the industry is and where it is going;

and is the one who has nurtured this business from the beginning, has cared for it like a child, and knows all of its idiosyncrasies. In other words, the founder "IS" the business, and no one knows it the way he or she does.

Furthermore, you as the founder of a business may have a difficult time giving up control of the business, the business that you have nurtured from its beginning. Even if you could do so, is there anybody who is capable of taking your place, or who has the foresight and vision to successfully drive the business over the next few decades so that you can collect residual income for the rest of your life?

No matter what happens, the founder will most likely be nervously checking in with the company's progress on a continuing basis, which does not really provide much of a basis for a relaxed retirement. One alternative where you as the founder would be free would be if the company had grown to such an extent that it literally no longer needed, or wanted, you any more. You hired people with skills that exceeded your own and phased yourself out of the business. To attract these people, you may have had to offer them ownership or stock in the company, reducing your percentage of ownership in the business. Such employee ownership does not occur very often, however, and in cases where it does, the founder's stock in the company may be so diluted from the company's continually raising more money to expand its operations and attract more high-level talent that

CREATING RESIDUAL INCOME

the founder may not end up with enough sellable stock or dividends to live on.

In all of the above scenarios, the pursuit of lifelong residual income is a difficult one at best, since the only way it can be achieved in the above examples is through the large accumulation of cash, real estate, or business equity. In other words, what you have been doing all of your life is trying to accumulate enough cash, or assets, so that you can live off the income from it for the rest of your life.

There is one type of business that a person can put his efforts into and work at long enough so as to create a solid residual income, yet never has to accumulate a large amount of cash or other assets in order to do so. This is through the concept of Network Marketing.

Network Marketing

Network Marketing offers one of the few opportunities to procure a lifelong income stream that does not first require the substantial accumulation of assets. A few other examples do exist, e.g., winning the lottery, where income keeps coming to you without regard to your own personal net wealth; patenting a product or process whereby a company pays you royalty fees for the right to produce and sell your product; or granting a company permission to use for a fee copyright or trademark material belonging to you. These examples do occur, and they do occur with some frequency, but they either involve an awful

NETWORK MARKETING: THE BEST OF THE BEST

lot of luck (as in winning a lottery) or an awful lot of hard work, technical knowledge, AND luck. In general these situations are beyond the scope of the average person, so he or she must look elsewhere to reach his or her dream.

Network Marketing offers the best opportunity to reach this goal of lifelong residual income and financial freedom without first having to accumulate large amounts of cash or other proprietary assets. It is perhaps the only method (other than winning the lottery) whereby a person with literally no job skills, no cash in the bank, no technical expertise, and no advanced education can set his mind to becoming financially independent and with literally nothing more than "the shirt on his back" and lots of motivation can achieve these goals of financial freedom and lifelong residual income.

Chapter 5.
Network Marketing

In order to understand Network Marketing, it is important to review traditional marketing.

Actually, we need to understand not only marketing but also sales and distribution for both traditional and Network Marketing approaches. In this chapter, the term "marketing" shall also include sales and distribution.

Traditional marketing

Traditional marketing involves goods and services originating with the manufacturer or service provider. These goods and services pass through several "middlemen," such as the national distributor, the local distributor or wholesaler, and the retailer, all of whom are compensated for their involvement. **Figure 3**, The distribution chain in traditional marketing, illustrates who the middlemen are and where they "fit" between the originator of goods and services and the end user or consumer. The number of middlemen varies from industry to industry. **Figure 4**, The expanded distribution chain in traditional marketing, illustrates that there are actually several levels of middlemen competing with each other. Before the consumer purchases the goods or services, he or she must be aware that they exist and must have the desire to purchase them. Once the desire to purchase them

```
Manufacturer or Service Provider
            │
            ▼
    National Distributor
            │
            ▼
Local Distributor or Wholesaler
            │
            ▼
         Retailer
            │
            ▼
         Consumer
```

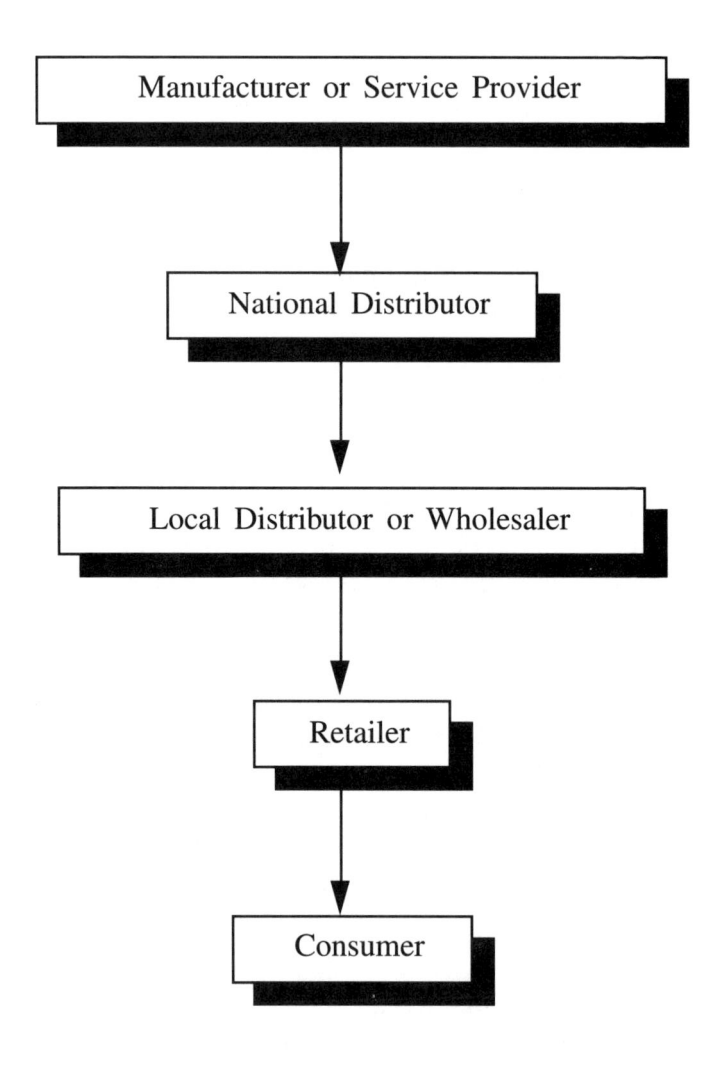

Figure 3. The distribution chain in traditional marketing.

NETWORK MARKETING

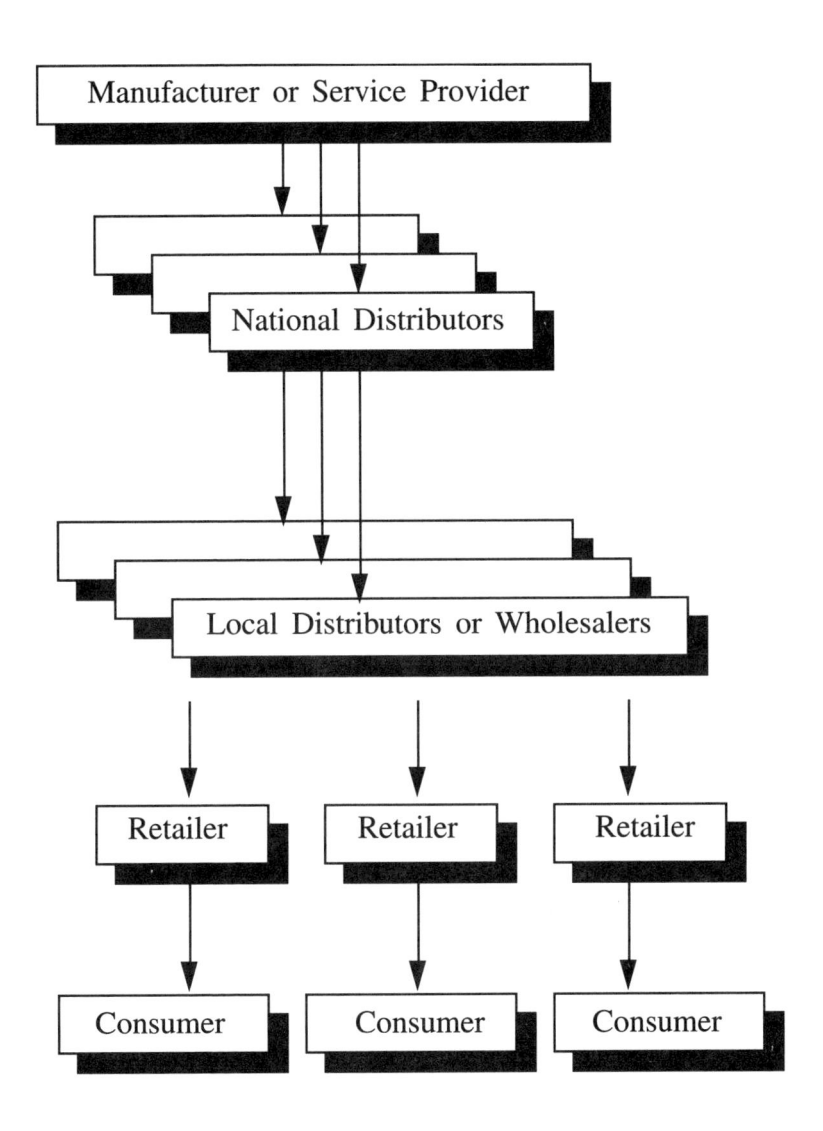

Figure 4. The expanded distribution chain in traditional marketing.

exists, the consumer locates and purchases them. For example,
> a consumer is browsing the shelves in a store (retail business) and sees a product that was advertised on television. The consumer purchases this product.

In this case, the television ad created the desire, or "demand pull," for this specific product. The retailer purchased the product from a local distributor or wholesaler and put it on the shelf to meet the consumer demand. The wholesaler purchased the product from a national distributor who purchased the product from the manufacturer.

The level of consumer desire for a product varies. In this example, the consumer saw the product while in a retail store and bought it. The store owner, or retailer, gets credit for properly placing the product so that the consumer sees it and for having the foresight even to carry the product. All manufacturers would like the desire for their product to be so great that the consumer would make a special trip to the store just to buy it.

In some cases, the manufacturer pays for essentially all of the advertising aimed at the consumer. The manufacturer also may direct some advertising at the middlemen to encourage them to purchase more of the product. Usually, the middlemen advertise and promote the product also, but they aim their efforts at their customers who are other middlemen. Their goal is to sell more of the product. The middlemen buy and sell many products from many manufacturers. They buy products in large quantities, store them in their warehouse, and take orders for the products (in smaller quantities than they purchase the products). Everyone involved profits by selling products, so they are all motivated to take steps to increase sales. In addition to advertising, steps used to increase product sales include the following:

Special pricing. Special pricing may be in the form of "reduced pricing for the month" or "buy five of this item and get one of this other item free" or "buy two of this item and get a third free."

Bundled product. Bundled product is where two or more different products, which would be used by the same consumer, are sold together at a price that is less than the sum of their separate prices. For example, in the computer software business, computer owners typically purchase utility programs to help them recover accidentally erased files and perform a whole assortment of other similar tasks. They also purchase "anti-virus" software to protect their data from software "viruses," the computer programs that damage data files when run. A very popular bundle in the 1990s was Symantec Corporation's *Norton Utilities for the Macintosh* bundled with *Symantec Anti-*

virus for the Macintosh. Consumers saved about 30% by purchasing the bundle as compared to buying each software package separately.

Spiffs. Spiffs are commissions paid directly to the salesperson, not the company that employs that salesperson. Spiffs sometimes are opportunities to earn or win vacations, TVs, tickets to a Super Bowl game, etc. As of the initial writing of this book, a promotion utilizing spiffs is being used by Intel Corporation, the world's largest manufacturer of microprocessors, to increase sales of its performance-boosting replacement microprocessors. For sales between April 3, 1995, and December 31, 1995, Intel Corporation is offering resellers a variety of prizes, travel packages, or cash (up to $10,000) in their "Quantum Leap Program" for those resellers who sell the Intel OverDrive® processors. These microprocessors would replace the older Intel 486 microprocessors and significantly improve performance, allowing older computers to remain useful for another year or two. The Intel OverDrive® processor is, and will continue to be, a very cost-effective solution for many companies and individuals. Resellers earn points for each Intel OverDrive® processor sold: one point for IntelDX2, eight points for IntelDX4, and 10 points for Pentium. Resellers need at least 50 points to earn prizes; at and above 250 points, resellers qualify for $1 cash per point or prizes; at or above

5,000 points they qualify for cash, prizes, or various travel packages. Intel limited the maximum cash payout because, as one Intel insider told us, the company had paid out amounts far in excess of $10,000 to many individuals in earlier spiff programs that were similar.

Co-op advertising. Co-op advertising is when a manufacturer or distributor pays for some of the cost of advertising. Sometimes it is based upon a percentage of the dollar amount of purchases during a period of time.

Whether a product or service, in traditional marketing, there are several middlemen involved. The middlemen are links in the "chain of distribution" from the manufacturer or service provider to the consumer. Each plays a significant role in the sale of product or services. The final cost of the goods or services, paid by the consumer, includes the actual cost of the product or service plus the advertising costs that created the market demand pull plus the costs of special pricing, bundling, spiffs, co-op advertising, and other promotional costs used to increase sales plus the profits paid to the middlemen for their role in the sales.

When you examine all of the costs in traditional marketing one fact jumps out at you—the fact that the actual cost of goods or services is only about 30% of the total price paid by the consumer. Of course this percentage will vary from industry to industry; however, the cost of marketing, sales, and distribution is almost always significantly more than the cost of the goods or services.

In each industry, the way that businesses operate will vary. Items such as shipping costs may or may not be included in pricing. Credit terms range from "payment in advance," to "due upon receipt" of goods or services, to payment due 30 days after the sale (also known as "Net 30 Days"), to any mutually agreed upon terms. In some cases, products are shipped "on consignment," which means the reseller pays only for product that has sold and returns unsold merchandise to the manufacturer. Return policies also vary from industry to industry. Return policy can range from a full refund for unsold merchandise, to a 25% restocking fee on returned goods, to "all sales final" with no product returns allowed. The markups, or multipliers used to calculate the selling price from the reseller's purchase cost, will also vary. These markups may be as small as 1 - 2%, or 300% or even higher, depending on the industry. Each industry has its own "terms of the trade." The terms of the trade have a great influence over the cost, and how readily available a product or service is, to the consumer.

In the example of the browsing consumer above, the consumer was aware of the product and had the desire to purchase the product. Creating the awareness and desire for the product is marketing. A general rule in marketing is that the consumers must see or hear an ad at least three times before they become aware of the product or service. Creating the desire, or demand pull, for a product takes not only a good product, but a lot of advertising. Maintaining demand pull for a product typically requires advertising on an ongoing basis. This advertising is incredibly expensive. Television ads can run over $1,000,000 per minute during major sports events such as a Super Bowl. Magazine ads range from a cost of tens of thousands of dollars for a full-page ad in a national publication to several hundred dollars for a small-circulation local publication. Other media such as radio or billboards are expensive, too. Remember, it is the manufacturer or service provider that creates "market demand pull" by advertising the product or service so that consumers will want to purchase it.

In the case of a product, the manufacturer also needs to invest heavily in producing the product to "fill up the pipeline." Each of the middlemen needs the product in stock to fill the anticipated orders. By the way, with new products or new companies, middlemen don't want to buy the product. They want it on consignment. In other words, they want the manufacturer to provide them with the product, but they don't want to pay for it until it is sold. They don't want to assume the risk of being caught with inventory that isn't selling in the event that the demand pull is not strong enough.

NETWORK MARKETING: THE BEST OF THE BEST

To summarize, in traditional marketing, goods or services originate at the manufacturer or service provider and are sold to distributors who sell to other distributors or retailers who sell to the consumer. The manufacturer or service provider creates demand pull through expensive advertising. Everyone in the chain of distribution profits from selling the goods or services. All of the expenses are paid for by the consumer. Most of the final amount paid for the goods or services by the consumer covers advertising and distribution costs, NOT the manufacturer's cost of goods or the service provider's cost of providing the actual services.

Network Marketing

Network Marketing is an alternative approach to the distribution and sales of goods and services. It combines "Networking" and "Marketing." "Networking" is the coming together of numbers of people who share information, resources, and support in a mutually beneficial way. "Marketing," in this context, refers to the movement of goods and services from the manufacturer or service provider to the end user.

In Network Marketing, the company that provides the product or services sold through the network of independent distributors is called the servicing corporation or Network Marketing company.

The servicing corporation does not create the demand pull for its goods or services through the use of expensive advertising in various media such as billboards, magazines and newspapers, and radio and television. The servicing organization usually does some advertising, but not very much. In Network Marketing, the independent distributor creates the "demand pull" for the products and services by informing and educating the consumer. The servicing corporation usually provides catalogs to the independent distributor for a minimal charge. Using the catalogs printed by the servicing corporation, an independent distributor sells the goods or services to the consumer, as well as other distributors that he or she has sponsored (i.e., recruited into the network). The independent distributor is also a consumer of the goods and or services that he or she distributes. Each independent distributor earns a bonus, commission, and/or profit based on the sales that he or she, and everyone that he or she sponsored, makes over a given period of time (e.g., one month). **Figure 5**, The distribution chain in Network Marketing, illustrates the flow of goods and services in Network Marketing.

In Network Marketing, as in traditional marketing, everyone who handles the sale of goods or services gets a profit for his or her involvement. There are middlemen in Network Marketing, but the cost to the consumer in most cases is less than through traditional distribution because there are considerably lower marketing and advertising costs, and the independent distributors who sell goods and services to other distributors typically get a very small profit from each sale. Their commissions, bonuses, and profits come

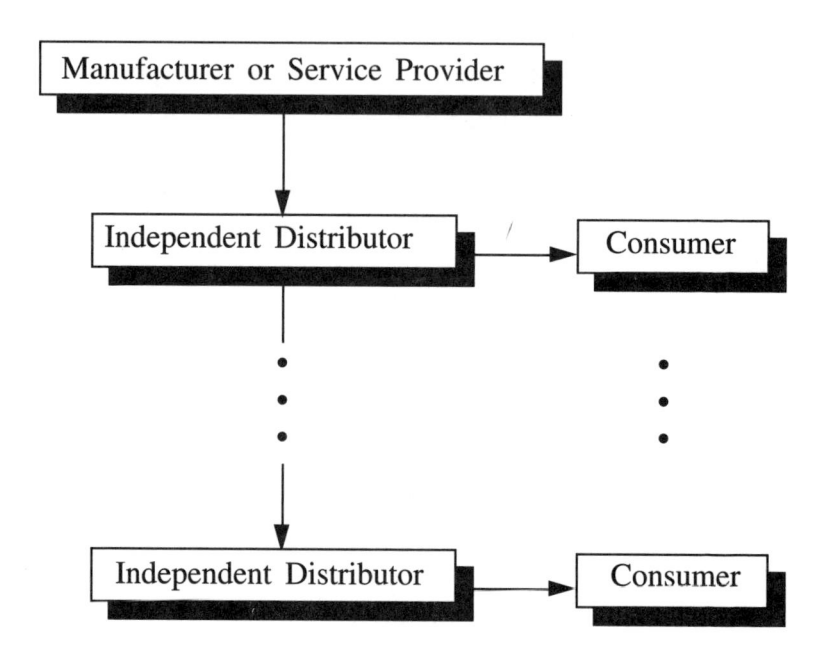

Figure 5. The distribution chain in Network Marketing.

from the servicing organization, which provides the goods and services to the independent distributors at wholesale prices. In traditional marketing, advertising and sales cost about 70% of the amount paid by the consumer. In Network Marketing, the total amount paid out to the distributors (in the form of bonuses, commissions, and profits) is usually several percent less, typically 60 to 65%. You might ask: Why is it only a few percent lower and not, say, 40% less? The reason is simple. To sell your goods and services, you must offer individuals an incentive to make the sale. If the incentive is too high, then no one will buy your goods and services because they aren't cost competitive. If the incentive is too low, then it will be difficult to find someone willing to sell and distribute them. Today, there are hundreds of Network Marketing companies. It has become a multi-billion-dollar-per-year industry, and many of the independent distributors are becoming millionaires.

Note: Many people have questioned whether Network Marketing is a legal business. In 1979, the Federal Trade Commission (FTC) investigated Amway and found it to be legal (1979 FTC Docket Number 9023). The FTC decision recognized the legitimate status of Network Marketing as a business opportunity. Furthermore, congressional legislation and the 1982 Tax Equity Fairness Responsibility Act recognized the "independent contractor" status of direct sellers.

NETWORK MARKETING: THE BEST OF THE BEST

John Fogg, Editor-in-Chief of *Upline*, a monthly journal written for the Network Marketing industry, says:

"IMAGINE:

What if there were a way for you to earn an income with a proven professional career

- that was affordable to start;
- that gave you creative control;
- that provides you the opportunity to be your own boss;
- that allows you to work part time or full time: when; where; and the way you choose; with the people you choose to work with;
- that educates and trains too;
- that was based on a proven, duplicatable system, that had already worked for tens of thousands of average people;
- where you could honestly earn what you were truly worth; and
- where with a little luck and lots of work, hitting the jackpot was truly possible?

There is a way!" ... NETWORK MARKETING.

NETWORK MARKETING

In a three-part article, *Why Network Marketing Is the Hope of the Future*, published in the January 1995 *Upline*, *The Journal for Network Marketing Sales Leaders*, Jim Rohn, Brian Tracy, and Paul Zane Pilzer share their insights on Network Marketing.

Jim Rohn, millionaire, author, and world-renowned motivational speaker, was asked to identify which one aspect of Network Marketing was absolutely the very best benefit for people. His answer: "What it makes of you rather than what you earn. And you can earn a great deal."[1] He goes on to say that the benefits include what you become, the skills you learn, the people you get to associate with, the people you meet, the training, the schooling, and the tutoring, all of which are far more valuable than the money.

Brian Tracy is the chief operating officer of a development company that has over $75 million in annual sales. He has traveled and worked in over 80 countries on six different continents and speaks four languages. He is one of the world's foremost sales, business, and success trainers. "Network Marketing is the opportunity to do well by doing good...." He goes on to say that "... The first-rate Network Marketing companies that sell high-quality products at competitive prices and offer opportunities for people to dramatically better their lives starting with very little represent one of the greatest parts of the American Dream."[2]

Paul Zane Pilzer is one of the world's most prominent economists, a professor and counselor to presidents, who has authored the best seller *Unlimited Wealth*, a book that explains why Network Marketing is such a good opportunity in today's global economy. He is also the author of *Should You Quit Before You're Fired?* He says, "More than any other single benefit, Network Marketing will lead the way in the twenty-first century...."[3]

Network Marketing has the potential to provide an individual with unlimited income, but it doesn't come immediately. Building a Network Marketing organization of your own takes time and a lot of effort. You need to sponsor and support many good people who believe in what they are doing as well as the quality, integrity, and price competitiveness of the servicing corporation's goods and services. When the organization you build is large enough, it can continue to grow without your involvement. That continued growth is a powerful vehicle for creating ever-increasing residual income. The growth is referred to as "duplication."

What is "duplication" in Network Marketing?

Duplication is when you sponsor or recruit persons into your Network Marketing organization who do the same thing that you do; in other words, they personally use the products or services, they sell the products or services retail and wholesale, and they sponsor others who do the same.

NETWORK MARKETING

Why is duplication so important?

Since there are only 24 hours in a day and seven days in a week, we are all limited by the fact that there are only 168 hours per week. You can't work more than 168 hours per week. If you are like most people, you need to use some of these hours to eat, sleep, and commute to and from work, and you probably need time to "unwind." If you get paid by the hour, no matter how much per hour you charge, there is a limit to how much you can make. Many professionals, including physicians and lawyers, have said that they reach a point where they ask themselves: Do I really want to "sell" all of these hours, or should I keep more for myself and my family?

Benjamin Franklin once observed that he had spent his first forty years turning his time into money and his second forty years turning his money back into time. Franklin had accumulated a large enough estate during the first four decades of his life to provide him with enough residual income to allow him to do whatever he wanted to do for the rest of his life. It's a lucky thing for all of us that he did!

Time is valuable. Today, someone with a lot of money usually doesn't have the time to enjoy it, and someone with a lot of time usually doesn't have much money. It is rare to have both money and the time to enjoy spending it. Network Marketing offers the potential for duplication that gives you a chance to have both.

The math behind duplication

Twos

If you sponsor two people and they sponsor two each, and they sponsor two each, ... it adds up as follows: the first level (below you) has two people, the second level has four people (two people in this level times two people that they each sponsor), the third level has eight people ... the tenth level will have 1,024 people.

This next paragraph is for all of the math wizards, looking into Network Marketing, who require it:

> The number of people at a given level below you is equal to the number of people sponsored by each person raised to the power of the level number below you. The actual equation is:

(Number of people at level "x") = (# of people sponsored by each)$^{(x)}$

> so the number of people in the first level below you is $2^1 = 2$, the number of people in the second level below you is $2^2 = 2 \times 2 = 4$, and the number of people in the third level below you is $2^3 = 2 \times 2 \times 2 = 8$. The number of people in the tenth level below you is equal to $2^{10} = 1,024$.

NETWORK MARKETING

Threes

If you sponsor three people and they sponsor three each, and they sponsor three each, ... it adds up as follows:

The first level below you has three people (3^1), the second level has nine people (3^2), the third level has 27 people (3^3) ... the tenth level will have 59,049 people.

The power of duplication

To see how powerful duplication can be, look at **Figure 6**, The power of duplication, and see how fast the numbers grow as you add to your downline. In this figure, the number of people sponsored by each person in your downline is listed across the top row. The left-hand column lists the level below you. The number of people at a specific level in your downline is found at the intersection of the number of people sponsored and the level. The total number of people in each group is shown on the bottom row.

The total number of people in your organization is the sum of you and all of the people in each level below you. When your organization is 10 levels deep (i.e., there are 10 levels below you) then the total number of people in your organization when everyone sponsors two each will be 2,047. When everyone sponsors 3 each, it will be 88,573. You can see how dramatically your organization increases in size when the number sponsored by each goes from two to three.

Figure 6. The power of duplication.

Level below you:	# of people sponsored by each person in your downline				
	2	3	4	5	6
you	1	1	1	1	1
1	2	3	4	5	6
2	4	9	16	25	36
3	8	27	64	125	216
4	16	81	256	625	1,296
5	32	243	1,024	3,125	7,776
6	64	729	4,096	15,625	46,656
7	128	2,187	16,384	78,125	279,936
8	256	6,561	65,536	390,625	1,679,616
9	512	19,683	262,144	1,953,125	10,077,696
10	1,024	59,049	1,048,576	9,765,625	60,466,176
Total in your organization:	2,047	88,573	1,398,101	12,207,031	72,559,411

When each person in your organization sponsors more than one person (and each sponsors the same number of people) you have a geometric progression. This illustrates the growth potential through duplication in Network Marketing.

Note: This is actually an oversimplification since not everyone in your organization will sponsor the same number of people.

When each person in your organization sponsors more than one person (and each sponsors the same number of people) you have a geometric progression. Figure 6. illustrates the growth potential through duplication in Network Marketing. *Note*: This is actually an oversimplification since not everyone in your organization will sponsor the same number of people.

Imagine what it would be like to have one hour of effort per week from each person in your downline. The 168-hour limit disappears. That is the power of duplication!

Network Marketing is built on the power of duplication.

The paradigm shift

With downsizing taking place in the Corporate World and many people seeking additional sources of income, greater financial stability, and freedom, there is a paradigm shift taking place and it is toward Network Marketing. We believe that this is a good place to position yourself for the future.

Why Network Marketing is the choice of the future

Market forces that are creating this paradigm shift toward Network Marketing are powerful and well-entrenched. These market forces are coming from all sectors of our global economy: product manufacturers, consumers, displaced/laid-off workers, entrepreneurs, retirees, new product developers and marketers, and governments. The forces creating this marketing shift are so strong and so pervasive throughout our entire economy that the potential business opportunities resulting from this shift in behavior will overshadow, in our opinion, most other business opportunities during the next several decades. It represents the choice of the future for many sectors of the global economy:

Product manufacturers

Network Marketing is without doubt the quickest, easiest, and most efficient way for most companies to distribute their goods and services. It is a cost-effective, reliable way to get product to the marketplace and is being used by many corporate giants throughout the country. It is also a useful medium to try out new products and involves a much lower degree of risk for product introduction than most traditional marketing programs. It is a shift that is rapidly changing the way many companies do business today. AT&T, for example, has lost more than a quarter of its long-distance market share to two of its competitors, MCI and Sprint, both of which have used Network Marketing as a means of signing up new customers.

Consumers

Consumers think Network Marketing is the "greatest invention since sliced bread," because not only can they buy high-quality products or services at, or below, traditional prices, but they can, in effect, buy many of these products or services at no cost, or even at a profit, if they themselves are involved in the business opportunity and receive commission/bonus checks from the company for purchases made by their downline. In addition to cost, they do not even have to get into their cars to drive to the store to do their shopping. In many cases, they can order their goods or sign up for services directly from the Network Marketing company (assuming the Network Marketing company offers this service) and have their goods shipped directly to them at home. It is a "no-lose" situation for the consumer.

Displaced workers
The Corporate World has undergone a major change and will probably never again offer the security and lifelong job opportunities that were available several decades ago. To augment their incomes and their financial security, many families are looking into Network Marketing opportunities. A careful, exploratory beginning can lead to a fulfilling, lifelong residual income. Corporate pensions and other traditional retirement plans are not nearly as secure as they once were. This means that people must become more innovative and develop their own strategies for retirement—a goal that can be obtained through the residual income created from Network Marketing.

NETWORK MARKETING: THE BEST OF THE BEST

Entrepreneurs

Perhaps no other group can have as much fun with Network Marketing as the entrepreneur who believes in the freedom, income potential, and sheer excitement of building a powerful income-producing organization with little risk and literally no borrowed money. Network Marketing is truly one of the great bastions of free enterprise where anyone can participate and become as rich and successful as he or she wants.

Network Marketing is a call to the "free spirit" in each one of us, one that is being heard around the world as former totalitarian societies open up, creating explosive growth in personal freedom, lifestyle choices, and income opportunities.

Retirees

Many individuals who either are on the verge of retiring or have already retired, no longer are able to maintain that standard of living which they had been accustomed to during their working years. This is a very troubling experience that is occurring throughout all segments of our economy. To augment their incomes, many retired individuals are turning to Network Marketing. Besides their increased earnings, they are also finding that they are making new friends, getting out more, and becoming actively involved in community affairs. Best of all, they feel great about themselves because they are doing good by helping others with similar problems. Many are also finding that their lives are becoming more exciting as their downline organization grows and affords travel to various parts of the world for organizational conferences, seminars, etc. To some retirees, Network Marketing is more of a hobby than anything else, but to others it is their only opportunity to become self sufficient and to live their lives with a certain degree of dignity.

New product developers and marketers
New product development can be incredibly expensive, as can the costs associated with getting these products out into the marketplace. Large companies may spend tens of millions of dollars getting new products introduced into the market and then spend equal amounts on advertising budgets. Network Marketing is a "dream come true" for these people because very few costs are associated with new product introductions, as the chain of distribution is already established and consumer acceptance is much more predictable.

Governments
Most governments in the world would like to see the living standards of their citizens improved. This is especially true in the newly formed democratic societies where living standards are often dismally low and quality products are practically nonexistent. What better way is there to raise living standards, introduce badly-needed consumer products, and ignite the spirit

of free enterprise than to allow Network Marketing companies to flourish within their borders? Again, it is a "no-lose" situation.

The paradigm shift away from traditional marketing and toward Network Marketing is taking hold around the world with a vengeance. It is not a passing fad, nor is it just another marketing scheme dreamed up by Madison Avenue. It is a reality that benefits almost everyone it touches. We are witnessing, within our own lifetimes, one of the biggest distribution paradigm shifts ever to occur—made possible in part by the equally powerful shift taking place in the computer industry. High technology has made Network Marketing so simple and so efficient that literally anyone can take advantage of its opportunities today and become as successful as he or she wants. The window of opportunity has never been wider.

Network Marketing is an incredible opportunity because of the paradigm shift taking place. As you consider getting into this industry, your next step is to select a Network Marketing servicing corporation.

---

1. *Upline*, January 1995, p. 8.
2. Ibid., p. 11.
3. Ibid., p. 14.

Chapter 6.
Selecting a Network Marketing Company

Once you have decided that the Network Marketing business is for you, the next important step is to determine which company most closely meets your needs and expectations. It is VERY important to find a company that you feel comfortable with and one that offers the support and integrity needed to establish a long-term relationship—a key ingredient to the build-up of a strong business and a continuing flow of residual income throughout the lifetimes of you and your family. If, for example, you choose a company that offers huge immediate payouts within a very short time period and with minimal effort, you may end up, after a few years of hard work, with a company unable to fulfill its promises and on the verge of bankruptcy. Or you may find that there is no strong support system within the organization, as everyone is out to take advantage of quick profits, and little or no attention is paid to the long-term objectives of each individual.

When selecting the appropriate Network Marketing company, it is very important to ask yourself: What exactly are you looking for in this business? There are wildly speculative companies that have just started up, have no proven track record or product, and have presented you with projections that make even them blush with guilt. If you are looking for the possibility of a "quick kill" within a relatively short period of time, this may be the opportunity for you. However, there are so many potential traps and pitfalls that they can only be termed "speculative business ventures" at best. You may be lucky and hit upon a new Amway or Shaklee or some other highly successful business, but the odds are greatly against this ever happening, and chances are much more likely that you will end up with a company that is unable to pay its bills within a few years. It is not fun to wake up five years down the road after putting in many long hours of hard work and building up a successful business to find that the company is either out of business or has changed its marketing plan to such an extent that you are, in effect, out of business.

Network Marketing is without doubt one of the best and possibly most lucrative businesses to be in, but unless you choose your Network Marketing company wisely by focusing in on such characteristics as integrity and stability, rather than emotional appeals of "get rich quick" schemes, you are likely to be sadly disappointed.

When choosing a Network Marketing company for yourself, there are several broad criteria to follow that will help you determine whether the company meets your requirements for stability, integrity, and support. This list is not necessarily all inclusive, but it does represent the building blocks of a strong foundation for any business you may contemplate joining.

SELECTING A NETWORK MARKETING COMPANY

Strong management

A strong, credible management team that has proven integrity and high moral values is absolutely essential. Without an honest and strong management team in place, you might as well be going to Las Vegas and placing your future on the craps table. The "get rich quick" scheme may be absent, but in its place are stability, security, and better odds of a successful long-term business relationship.

Proven track record

This criterion is second only to that of strong management. While the past can never predict the future, it can certainly indicate to you what is important to the company and how successful its marketing program, products, and public acceptance have been, and it clearly shows the company is not a fly-by-night organization.

When choosing a company, you should generally limit yourself to those that have been in business for at least five years, and preferably longer. This is not a put-down to companies that are younger than five years because there may be some very good new ones attempting to gain a foothold in the marketplace, but finding one with at least five years of experience greatly reduces your odds of being disappointed and out of business, through no fault of your own, a few years down the road.

Debt-free finances

The company you choose should be financially secure and as nearly debt-free as possible. There is nothing that can bring a company down faster than a large debt. It becomes top heavy, grows too fast or too slowly, and is unable to pay off existing debt. The company falls like a house of cards, leaving all of its customers with nowhere to turn.

Long-term vision

The company must have a long-term vision of its future, well planned and thought out, that carries it beyond several decades and is committed to the well-being and development of its independent distributors. If it has no long-term goal and is only committed to its own well-being, rather than that of its distributors, forget it. It will not be around long enough for you to enjoy the residual income benefits that you have worked so hard to establish for your retirement. Distributors are the lifeblood of any Network Marketing company, and without full management commitment to their prosperity and well-being, the company will not make it.

Growth

As an offshoot to the long-term vision of the company, growth in terms of ever-widening markets, new product lines, and overseas expansion is essential to the overall long-term health of the company. A

SELECTING A NETWORK MARKETING COMPANY

company that sells only one (or just a few) product(s), in just one country, with no plans for expansion, will not be as attractive to prospective distributors nor will it offer the potential for rapid distributor/customer expansion as worldwide markets continue to grow. We are living in a global economy today, and any company that does not act accordingly is not worth your time. For many large corporations today, the bulk of their profits and growth are coming from overseas sales and not from sales within their own territorial borders.

Strong and diversified product line

You should never become a distributor for a company whose product line (1) you do not believe in; (2) you would never personally use; or (3) is so small that it could quickly become obsolete through competition or bad press. A good Network Marketing company should be built upon a foundation of solid high-quality products. People get interested in a Network Marketing company first because of its great products, and second because of its great marketing plan (i.e., opportunity to make money through using and moving its products and sponsoring others to do the same). A good, well-diversified product line will keep people loyal to the organization and will keep them continually buying products. As the word gets out, and people start telling their friends about the great product line, it is amazing how fast your organization will grow.

NETWORK MARKETING: THE BEST OF THE BEST

A Network Marketing company is only as good as its products. If the products are not good, the company itself will never succeed, even with the greatest marketing plan in the world. Choose a company that has the highest-quality products. You want a company whose products are of such high quality that even if no marketing plan existed for the company, you would still choose their products to buy for yourself, your family, and your friends.

Choose a company whose products are necessary and that are typically used or consumed every day by every family. Consumable products mean repeat purchases, and repeat purchases mean more money in your pocket. The products must be competitively priced and affordable. People shop around. They know the going prices. If the products are not competitively priced, they will go elsewhere to buy. The products must be conveniently purchased. The customer should be able to order product by phone. There should be no long waits, no inventory build-up requirements, and minimal personal purchase requirements. The company should have in place a 100% satisfaction guarantee policy whereby, if a customer is dissatisfied with a purchase or product for any reason, the company will reimburse that customer, no questions asked.

SELECTING A NETWORK MARKETING COMPANY

Low entry fee
Beware of the company that offers "pie-in-the-sky" rewards in exchange for your making exorbitant up-front product purchases. You definitely are helping someone make money, but do you really want to shell out, say, $3,000 for products that sit in your basement or garage for five years before you finally are lucky enough to have them all sold? It is not worth it. You should look for a company with minimal startup costs, e.g., under $200—easily affordable by practically anyone who wishes to participate in the program. Otherwise, you are drastically limiting your potential customer base.

Strong company-sponsored distributor training and support
Find a company that offers a strong training and support system. A strong company-sponsored training and support system is worth its weight in gold. It has been developed for one reason only—to assure those individuals who want to succeed in the business the surest, quickest, and most time-tested way to do so. Once you are plugged into this program, and are willing to follow through, your chances for success are greatly magnified, if not assured.

It is important to have a line of sponsorship between you and the company (your upline) that is committed to its own long-term success and that sets an example for you to follow. The company, as well as your upline, must provide the atmosphere and attitude for ongoing personal growth for you and the people in your organization. Self-development and personal growth should be primary goals. Making large amounts of money usually accompanies the attainment of these two goals.

It is important that your sponsor be truly committed to the business, thereby setting an example for you. His or her focus thus becomes your success. You want a sponsor who is willing to go the extra mile in helping you achieve your goals. He or she should be capable of helping the individuals in your organization develop personally in character and integrity. Remember that the sponsor you choose will be working for you.

The tools and materials your upline may have to share with you can be invaluable and can often speed up the time it takes for you to succeed. Training meetings and materials such as videotapes, audiotapes, and literature can all assist in building your business.

Marketing plan

The company must offer a marketing plan that is fair and equitable to everyone. There must never be any risk of being hurt financially. The plan must be profitable for everyone at every level and yet must offer unlimited earning potential for those who desire it. Network Marketing is perhaps one of the few great remaining opportunities where the average person

SELECTING A NETWORK MARKETING COMPANY

with no special education or background can amass a fortune through lots of determination and hard work, and the company must always make this opportunity available to anyone who wishes to pursue it.

There are many Network Marketing companies in business today and these criteria help to sort through them. Use these criteria when you are selecting a Network Marketing company. The Network Marketing company that you choose today will greatly affect your chances for success tomorrow.

Chapter 7.
The Best of the Best in Network Marketing

Knowing what to look for in selecting a servicing corporation or Network Marketing company, we set out to find some that we could recommend in this book. After investigating many Network Marketing companies, we found that most are based on one or two product lines. With a few exceptions, most Network Marketing companies are relatively young (i.e., they were started in the past five years). Some were just getting started. Some of the companies are no longer in business. Some are based on obscure products that people are not already using on a regular basis. A few require new distributors to make large initial purchases in order to get competitive pricing. Some are selling product at very high prices—i.e., several times the normal "street" price for a similar product. Some require substantial monthly purchases in order for commissions to be paid.

In analyzing various Network Marketing companies in business today, and in matching them to the criteria that we set forth in Chapter 6 regarding what to look for in a Network Marketing company, we reached the conclusion that Amway Corporation offers the best opportunity to the individual who is seeking to break away from the Corporate World and establish his or her own business organization—the best opportunity based upon our basic parameters of company stability, integrity of management, durable track record, and strong company and upline support. No other company that we have researched can match Amway's achievements and dedication to these principles.

There are many good Network Marketing servicing corporations available today that are excellent companies dedicated to the prosperity of their distributors. But this chapter is about the one company that stands above the rest. It is about the company that perfected the Network Marketing concept and has gone on to become the leader—the one that others try to emulate. It is about the one company where, if you work hard for a few years at developing a good organization and helping others do the same, you never have to worry about life-long residual income, because the company is extremely well run and will be around for as long as you and your family are. You will never be working alone, because the Amway support system is truly an amazing feature—one that has never been replicated by any other organization.

There are many reasons why we have chosen Amway as the best of the best in Network Marketing. One of the less obvious reasons is the feeling that you get when your organization has grown to such an extent that free time allows you to travel anywhere in the world—meeting Amway distributors wherever you go and, should you feel so moved, adding new legs in whichever countries you choose. Amway is represented in more countries than any other servicing corporation in the world. Another reason is the moment someone asks you to come up onto the stage to explain your secrets of success and why you are proud to represent one of the truly amazing success stories in America's history. The list goes on and on ... and as you personally grow and as you steadily come to realize the power of the Amway success story, you begin to realize the distance between this company and all of the rest that in one way or another owe their origins to the BIG ONE. Amway was one of the original pioneers in the Network Marketing industry and has always been the leader in excellence for those who follow. It has also been the most successful and widely-respected role model in the industry. The potential to build a successful business today with Amway is probably more possible than at any other time in history. As international markets open up, as new products are developed and marketed, and as the world turns more toward Network Marketing and away from traditional marketing strategies, the opportunities literally become unlimited. It pays to work with the best if you are planning a long-term commitment to the paradigm shift that is currently transforming marketing philosophies throughout the world.

NETWORK MARKETING: THE BEST OF THE BEST

Let's consider some of our criteria with Amway in mind:

Management

Amway's management is absolutely second to none. It was started by two of the greatest entrepreneurs in America's history, Rich DeVos and Jay Van Andel, and is now under the guidance of each family's second generation, who have been preparing for years to accept this responsibility. Their track record is tried and true, their success has been astounding. The company was founded in 1959, and sales have grown continuously since then, reaching over $5.3 billion in 1994. Its leaders are committed to producing the highest-quality products available and have consistently demonstrated unyielding loyalty and support to its independent distributors. The management is without equal anywhere in the industry.

Company stability

Amway is debt free. The number of independent distributors has grown every year. More and more countries are being added to the roster of potential customer bases. Product line keeps expanding, innovative manufacturing processes continue to be implemented, and distribution channels continue to expand and become more efficient and user friendly. Its leaders are committed to producing high-quality products that are environmentally sensitive. Amway produces more than 400 of its own products. In June

1995, more than 60 U.S. and 37 international patents had been issued for Amway products, and 20 U.S. and 40 international patents were pending. In Michigan alone, Amway operates out of more than 80 buildings covering over 3,800,000 square feet of offices, space for manufacturing, research, and distribution, and other support facilities for more than 5,000 employees. These facilities stretch for about one mile along Fulton Street, which is referred to by some as the "Miracle Mile." In fact, Amway is the largest exporter of goods to Japan in the (auto manufacturing) state of Michigan. Amway is shipping over 350 million pounds of products to over 70 countries and territories each year.

If ever a company in America's history represented stability, Amway is it. Stability is at the heart of a successful Network Marketing company, because the goal of most distributors is to acquire a lifelong income stream for themselves and for their families—an achievement that can only be realized in this sort of environment.

Company and upline support

There is no company that offers its independent distributors more company support, leadership, and direction than Amway. The almost legendary code of ethics and principles of honesty, conduct, and fair play began with the original founders of the company and have continued to its present-day leaders. These values have created a rock-solid foundation of high moral values and integrity that permeate throughout the entire

NETWORK MARKETING: THE BEST OF THE BEST

organization and create a backdrop for success. These values start at the top and work their way through every line of sponsorship. They can be felt at every meeting and can be sensed from any of the numerous audiotapes, videotapes, books, etc., available for anyone who wishes to use them. Rich DeVos, the cofounder of Amway, states "... unless you have a set of positive values at the very core of your life, your goals will be inadequate and untrustworthy."[1]

This support from the top translates into strong upline support. In Amway, the company has creatively managed to capture the power of synergism, where group energies and efforts produce much greater results than individual efforts. Therefore, it is fundamental to the Amway success plan that the new distributor become a "partner" with his upline. This teaches him the ropes of the business, the power of duplication, and the value of working through an already-proven success plan which, when followed, will almost certainly assure success.

This support system is truly one of the company's most remarkable features and is probably the main reason that Amway has produced so many millionaires over the years. For the individual entrepreneur who is trying to become established in the Network Marketing business and who is willing to work within a time-tested method of proven success, there is no match. The guidance, the support system, and the plan are all in place. The only step left for the individual is to decide to jump in and ride the crest of the wave to success.

Product diversity and integrity

Amway offers a wide variety of products known throughout the world as the best money can buy. The company manufactures about 400 of its own products and distributes through its Personal Shopper and other specialty catalogs over 6,500 other name-brand products and services. Its cleaning products contain only biodegradable surfactants and are not tested on animals. It uses packaging containing recycled materials whenever possible—including "packing peanuts" that, instead of being made from polystyrene, are made from cornstarch, a material that dissolves completely in water and is not a threat to the environment. Most of Amway's products are in a concentrated form, which reduces packaging material and results in less solid waste in our landfills (plus provides a cheaper per use cost to the consumer).

According to Amway's environmental mission statement, the company recognizes its responsibility in promoting sound environmental stewardship and recognizes that the proper use and management of the world's resources must be the responsibility of individuals and industry alike. The company is a firm believer in practicing what it preaches and has won numerous awards in recognition of its sound and often before-its-time environmental practices. These commitments were made three decades ago, and on June 5, 1989, Amway received the United Nations Environment Programme's Award for Achievement and the United Nations insignia pin for outstanding work to protect the environment.

Because Amway carries such a diverse and high-quality line of products, the attractiveness of the program to prospective distributors becomes even more compelling. The products are mostly consumable, everyday products that are used by almost everybody. The company has more than 250 research and development scientists and 150 quality assurance personnel who are continually looking for ways to develop new products and improve existing ones. Good product diversity is key to a stable and growing company, and Amway certainly leads the pack.

Foreign markets

Amway is the leader here. Its international expansion already covers the globe and is represented in over 70 countries and territories. About two-thirds of Amway's sales are derived from overseas markets. If you like to travel, if you like a little adventure and excitement, and if you like the possibilities of opening new markets with a highly-respected company to back you up, then here is your opportunity. No other Network Marketing company can make this kind of offer with the support and guidance Amway has to offer.

The entrepreneurial spirit is exploding in many of the former communist countries, and what better way to utilize this pent-up energy and demand than to work with one of the largest, most widely respected, financially-secure Network Marketing companies in the world? When Amway first opened for business in Hungary in June 1991, it sold 35,000 sales kits during the first month of operation and more than 3,000 people passed through the pickup center in Budapest the first day! Similar stories are occurring throughout Eastern Europe. The potential for tapping into these business opportunities overseas is tremendous and in many instances is just beginning to be realized. The economy is global, the time is right, and Amway is presenting this opportunity on a "silver platter" to anyone with the foresight to take advantage of it.

Vision

The future of Network Marketing offers tremendous opportunities for those who see the paradigm shift taking place. The trend is obvious and is entrenching itself within all marketing sectors. The continued growth in Network Marketing is fueled by the entrepreneurial explosion taking place throughout the world today and the yearning of people for freedom over their lives and the chance to control their own destinies. Amway's vision is clearly a reflection of the realities taking place around the world, and it is positioning itself to remain the leader for many decades to come. It pays to stay with the best because people like to associate with winners, not losers. It is no wonder that companies like MCI, General Electric, Panasonic, IBM, Coca Cola, and Northwest Airlines

NETWORK MARKETING: THE BEST OF THE BEST

are turning to Amway to market their products and services, because they have the vision to see that Amway will be the Network Marketing leader 20 years down the road and that Amway will be the most respected Network Marketing company to represent their company and products. They could turn to any one of a number of Network Marketing servicing organizations for this task, but the one that they are choosing and the one that they consider to be the best of the best is Amway. With over 12,500 employees worldwide, 2,000,000 independent distributors, and its long-standing commitment to quality in all aspects of business, it is no wonder why. The company radiates a positive can-do image that is reflected in the energy and enthusiasm of its distributor force.

THE BEST OF THE BEST IN NETWORK MARKETING

Some other companies that utilize Amway's distribution network are:

Adidas	Mars Candy
Avia	Memorex
Bass Shoes	Nabisco
Chrysler	Pepperidge Farm
Creamette	Philips
Firestone	Porsche
Florsheim	Quaker
Ford	Sanyo
Franklin Quest	Seiko
Frito-Lay	Sharp
General Mills	Spalding
General Motors	Sylvania
Grolier Publishing	United Airlines
IBM	Warner's
Kellogg's	Waterford Crystal
L.A. Gear	Whirlpool
Levi Strauss	Wilson
London Fog	Zenith
Magnavox	

The entrepreneur should pay attention to the way Amway is viewed around the world. For his own financial interests—direct income, residual income, stability, etc.—he should note with an open mind what other respected international marketers and business leaders have already concluded.

NETWORK MARKETING: THE BEST OF THE BEST

Other Amway advantages

- It has minimal startup costs.
- It is portable—it can be done almost anywhere in the world.
- It is simple to understand and explain to others. It can be shown on a cocktail napkin.
- It requires no mandatory monthly purchases.
- It offers the opportunity to order directly from the company (via a toll-free 800 number) and have the product shipped directly to you.
- It offers that, in the event of your death, your organization can be willed or transferred to whomever you wish.
- It is a home-based business that you operate from your house or apartment.
- It is a cash business with no accounts receivable.
- It encourages strong ideals and lasting friendships.
- It offers a 100% money-back guarantee for both the consumer and the distributor on all products.
- It has a strong code of ethics that begins with the Golden Rule.
- It has worldwide recognition and respect.

- It offers low-cost business, health, life, and travel insurance to its distributors and their families.
- It offers a special international inquiries department as well as a product information services department.
- It offers a proven support system of training materials.

Recognizing that Amway is a leader in the Network Marketing business, we set out to find some success stories. In Chapter 8 you can gain insight from the comments of those who have already succeeded as Amway distributors. In the final chapter, Chapter 9, we will tell you how to get started in this business and give you some strategies for success.

---

1. Rich DeVos, *Compassionate Capitalism*, Plume (Penguin Books), 1994, p. 54.

Chapter 8.
Profiles of Success

Quotes from people who are successful in Amway

Amway has done much for many people who have gone into the Network Marketing business. Before you read their comments, it is helpful to understand the level of achievement that these individuals and couples have reached so, next to their names, we have included their title or "level of accomplishment" according to Amway's method of recognition.

Recognition within Amway

In the Amway business, people are recognized for their success and accomplishments. As their organization and their monthly business revenues grow larger, they are presented with pins that signify their level of achievement. Pins are given for Sales Achievement, Sales Consistency and Outstanding Achievement, and for various levels of sales revenues. These pins are usually presented by the upline sponsor or Direct Distributor.

As their success continues, they are further recognized with pins that signify their accomplishment: Silver Producer, Direct Distributor, Ruby Direct Distributor, Pearl Direct Distributor, Emerald Direct Distributor, Diamond Direct Distributor, Executive Diamond Direct Distributor, Double Diamond Direct

Distributor, Triple Diamond Direct Distributor, Crown Direct Distributor, and finally the highest level of achievement, Crown Ambassador Direct Distributor. These higher-level pins are presented by the Amway Corporation.

Here are some comments about this business from people who have succeeded in it:

"What I first saw in this concept, was the ability to duplicate my efforts many times over in order to create residual income that most people only dream of attaining at the end of a long career in the form of retirement income. I saw this vehicle, called 'Networking,' as a prudent investment in my future. It would short-circuit the long haul of 40 years of labor by four to five years of smart effort utilizing the leverage of time and money without risk." David and April Humphrey - Executive Diamond Direct.[1]

"My experience is that we can teach people how to dream big and how to think right. The keys are perseverance and consistent work." Cecilia Karasz - Diamond Direct.[2]

"Through the years, our success has been built on the idea that we just show people how simple achievement can be when they tap into this system—a system which has been proven time after time." Terry and Judy Argante - Triple Diamond Direct.[3]

PROFILES OF SUCCESS

"When you take financial pressure and a job out of your life there's not a lot else to worry about!" Mitch and Diedre Sala - Diamond Direct.[4]

"We believe that Network Marketing is just now beginning to explode. What the leaders in Networking have achieved is fantastic, but it is just a prelude to what lies ahead." Frank and Jo Bortz - Diamond Direct.[5]

"A wise man once said that there are only three things to know about to get what you want. One, decide what you want. Two, decide what you are willing to give up to get it. Three, go for it." Vince and Laurita Berland - Diamond Direct.[6]

"Unlike any other business, this one rewards you for productivity.... If you follow this system and never give up, you WILL succeed." Tom and Caryn Avelsgaard - Diamond Direct.[7]

"Our lifestyle today allows us extensive travel to other countries and gives us options, such as getting up when we're finished sleeping, not needing to answer to a boss, being free in a free country, and being able to offer the same opportunity to others." Peter and Angie Ross - Diamond Direct.[8]

"The best part of Network Marketing is that you have so many tools available to help anyone at whatever pace they want to move." Mick and Jenny Clark - Diamond Direct.[9]

"The greatest help was the tools.... I've heard the phrase, 'Cake without eggs ain't cake!' This system works best when you use all of the ingredients—books, tapes, and meetings. We decided quickly that we didn't need to reinvent the wheel. We became good copycats. In fact, this is one of the few businesses in the world where you actually get paid very well for plagiarism!" Bob and Sue Covino - Diamond Direct.[10]

"Executive Diamond enables us to be free to do what we want to do, go where we want to go, and not answer to any man, and now we have the income to enjoy it. This is truly the best way of life." Jack and Rita Daughery - Executive Diamond Direct.[11]

"What matters most, is not so much how you got to be the way you are now, but what you do with the opportunities in front of you. This business can be built by anyone who has a big enough dream and is willing to do what works. Sometimes we make Network Marketing into something so difficult and complex. It doesn't have to be that way. It's a simple business. When you understand how simple it really is, you are on your way to success." Colombo and Karen DiSalvatore - Diamond Direct.[12]

PROFILES OF SUCCESS

" ... One of the greatest things about Network Marketing is that you have so much support built in to the system. You don't have to have years of experience and you don't have to be wealthy. The secret is to point to the people in this business who are already successful. Once you understand this principle, you stop worrying about being too young, too old, too inexperienced or too anything." Brad and Vera Doyle - Diamond Direct.[13]

"Networking is available to anyone who desires to make a better life for himself or herself. It works. We have seen what a person can do through networking too many times to believe any other way. The best part is that this business has even more opportunities today than ever before. How many other businesses can say that?" Hal and Susan Gooch - Double Diamond Direct.[14]

"The main thing we had to learn was how to have faith. We had been brought up with the mentality that there was security in having a job. Sometimes we let all the distractions take our eyes off the business and back to the short-term solution. Once Connie and I started working the business together, however, we began to see some results. Even when things didn't happen as quickly as we wanted them to, we just kept going." Gator and Connie Strong - Executive Diamond Direct.[15]

"So many people have simply stopped dreaming about having enough time and money to enjoy life. We have a system that works, as a quick glance through Profiles of Success will prove, and people can find networking heroes who are from every walk of life—truck drivers, musicians, physicians, even dairy farmers from Australia. Getting a dream of financial freedom is the common thread." John and Denise Hargreaves - Diamond Direct.[16]

"The best part is that we are a part of such a positive environment. Network Marketing has become the wave of the future. It's literally exploding all over the world. The people who get involved today have such an unlimited opportunity." Don and Janet Held - Diamond Direct.[17]

"The problem is often that people don't seize opportunities. So many people never get anywhere in life because, when opportunity knocks, they are out in the backyard looking for four-leaf clovers. It doesn't have to be that way, certainly not with this business opportunity." Jim and Bev Kinsler - Diamond Direct.[18]

"Financial freedom is more wonderful than you can imagine. Economic security takes an unbelievable pressure off your shoulders. Best of all, anyone with a big enough dream can use Network Marketing to achieve this goal." Jim and Kelly Law - Diamond Direct.[19]

"We were looking for a way to achieve a truly free and independent lifestyle. A doctor's time is never his own.... It is a great thrill for us today to see others reach their goals and dreams. We feel we have been able to touch more lives in more meaningful ways than we ever could have done in a fast-paced medical practice." Greg and Laurie Duncan - Double Diamond Direct.[20]

"... We owe our success to our upline for their support and guidance, and for setting an example for us in their personal and business lives.... We want everyone to know that dreams do come true! Our dreams have come true, and we know this is only the beginning. Our future is so bright we have to wear shades!" Scott and Cris Harimoto - Diamond Direct.[21]

"Nobody can tell me there's a better business opportunity than Amway. I had nine and a half years of college and a $30,000 debt when I started my optometry practice. To me that is a tremendous price to pay for a mediocre lifestyle. Amway changed that scenario very quickly, without financial risk.... We are holding freedom in our hands. There is no restriction to the freedom of attaining financial, emotional, physical, and spiritual prosperity." Theron and Darlene Nelsen - Executive Diamond Direct.[22]

NETWORK MARKETING: THE BEST OF THE BEST

"The best thing of all is that we can share our lifestyle with others. By going out and sharing the opportunity with people we can open up a whole new world to them—a world that isn't controlled by time and money or what some corporate entity wants done, a world where people can choose the life they want and can achieve their dreams." Mike and Michi Woods - Diamond Direct.[23]

"We never imagined, even in our wildest dreams, what was available at Diamond. Our story is a simple message ... to just get started and not quit! Whatever you do, base your decisions on information you receive from winners and doers, not whiners and doomsdayers. Listen to people who are making this business work. Follow the system, and you can make it happen!" John and Maureen Minaudo - Diamond Direct.[24]

"With layoffs, business closings, the economic ups-and-downs and people with little security, more and more people are looking for something that provides a tremendous income potential with little capital risk. The time has never been better for Network Marketing. That's why we are so excited about helping others grow." Jerrel and Kay Shaw - Triple Diamond Direct.[25]

"Network Marketing offers the potential opportunity to not only provide a permanent, self-sustaining income, but also a way to get past time constraints through the ingenious concept of leverage. Leverage simply means putting a little of what you have with a little of what other people have, and then accomplishing something powerful together that you could never do all by yourself. Leveraging is one of the keys to today's economic growth in almost any area of the market place, and it is one of the most important elements in the exciting, powerful world of networking." Glenn and Pam Shoffler - Diamond Direct.[26]

"It might sound trite, but we grew fast by concentrating on helping other people reach whatever goals they wanted to reach. We came across so many people who were literally afraid to dream, or maybe their dreams had died. We found that if we loved them enough the dream could be ignited again. The people seemed to sense that we really were concerned about their success and that we were willing to put in the time and effort to help them reach their goals and dreams. Because we had these feelings right from the start, our business grew very quickly." Dan and Bunny Williams - Crown Ambassadors.[27]

"The business has given us a lifestyle that most people will only dream about and the ability to help others achieve it too." Ray and Betty Storer - Diamond Direct.[28]

"Together we all take responsibility for each other. The new person is really the one who makes it happen. We consider it our job to help you as a new distributor get from where you are in the business, to where you want to go. Your upline is an important part of your life. They are not your boss, they are just people who have been where you are and who want to help you get to where they are, so that you can turn around and help other new people who are where you were, to get to where they want to go. It's that simple. A win-win situation." Bill and Peggy Britt - Crown Ambassadors.[29]

No other corporation has produced as many success stories as Amway.

If your line of sponsorship publishes "Profiles of Success" and you would like to share one or more of these success stories with others, please send your request, along with your name, address, and phone number to Sunrise Press, Inc., Attention: David Stone, and we'll try to include a quote or two in future printings of this book. Our address is listed inside the back cover.

---

1 "Profiles of Success" published by World Wide Dreambuilders 1994.

PROFILES OF SUCCESS

2. "Profiles of Success" published by Network 21.
3. "Profiles of Success" published by Internet Services Corporation 1978, 1993, p.23.
4. "Profiles of Success" published by Network 21.
5. "Profiles of Success" published by Internet Services Corporation 1978, 1993, p.47.
6. "Profiles of Success" published by Internet Services Corporation 1978, 1993, p.37.
7. "Profiles of Success" published by Internet Services Corporation 1978, 1993, p.27.
8. "Profiles of Success" published by Network 21.
9. "Profiles of Success" published by Internet Services Corporation 1978, 1993, p.73.
10. "Profiles of Success" published by Internet Services Corporation 1978, 1993, p.81.
11. "Profiles of Success" published by World Wide Dreambuilders 1994.
12. "Profiles of Success" published by Internet Services Corporation 1978, 1993, p.101.
13. "Profiles of Success" published by Internet Services Corporation 1978, 1993, p.107.
14. "Profiles of Success" published by Internet Services Corporation 1978, 1993, p.137.

15. "Profiles of Success" published by World Wide Dreambuilders 1994.

16. "Profiles of Success" published by Internet Services Corporation 1978, 1993, p.155.

17. "Profiles of Success" published by Internet Services Corporation 1978, 1993, p.173.

18. "Profiles of Success" published by Internet Services Corporation 1978, 1993, p.203.

19. "Profiles of Success" published by Internet Services Corporation 1978, 1993, p.213.

20. "Profiles of Success" published by World Wide Dreambuilders 1994.

21. "Profiles of Success" published by World Wide Dreambuilders 1994.

22. "Profiles of Success" published by World Wide Dreambuilders 1994.

23. "Profiles of Success" published by World Wide Dreambuilders 1994.

24. "Profiles of Success" published by Internet Services Corporation 1978, 1993, p.273.

25. "Profiles of Success" published by Internet Services Corporation 1978, 1993, p.329.

26. "Profiles of Success" published by Internet Services Corporation 1978, 1993, p.333.

PROFILES OF SUCCESS

27. "Profiles of Success" published by Internet Services Corporation 1978, 1993, p.379.
28. "Profiles of Success" published by Network 21.
29. "Profiles of Success" published by World Wide Dreambuilders 1994.

Reserved for future Profiles of Success

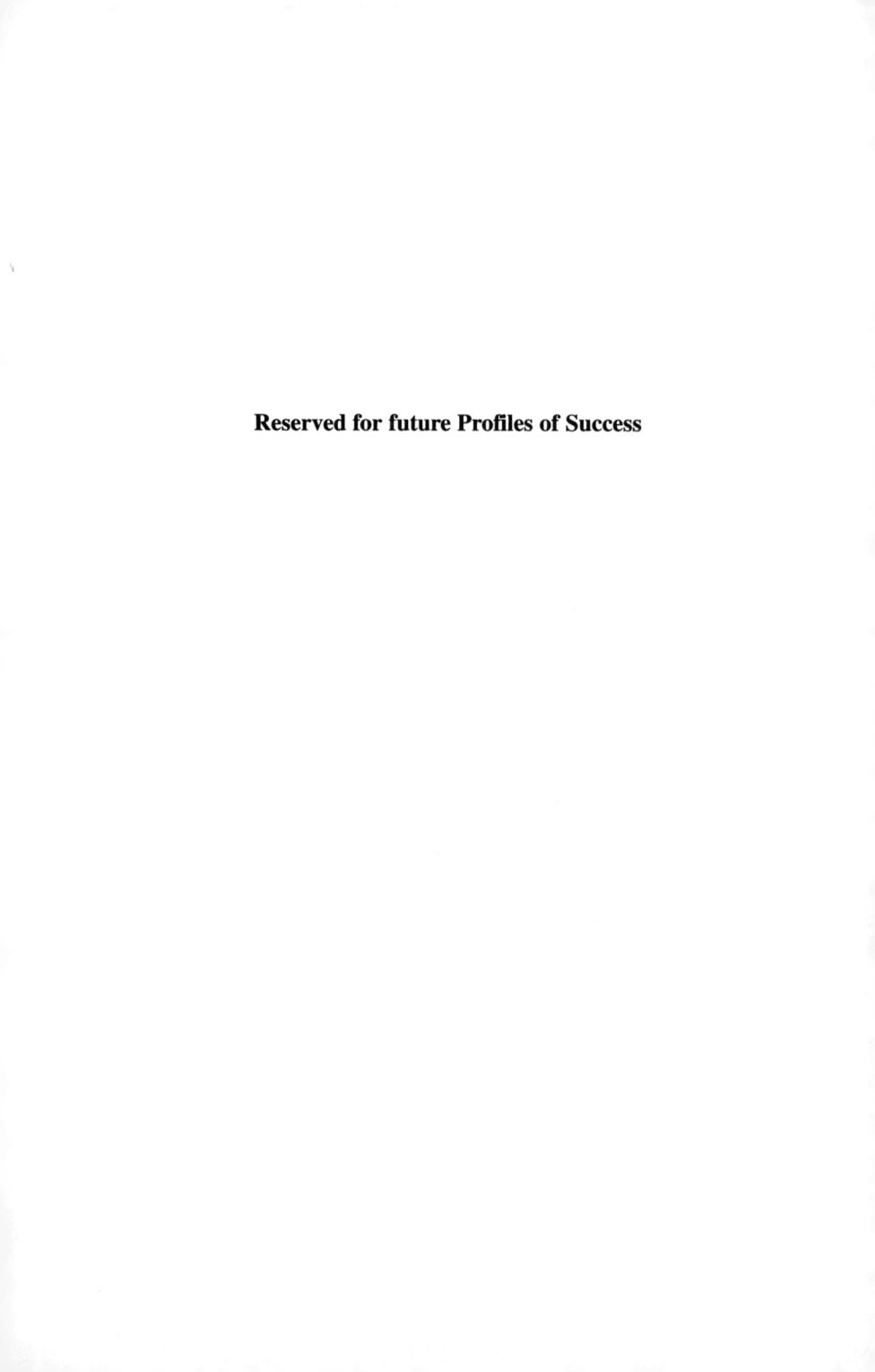

Reserved for future Profiles of Success

Chapter 9.
How to Get Started in This Business

There are several steps that you should take before making the commitment to get into this business:

- Review "the plan" at least three times. The Amway Business Review—Corporate Report / Sales and Marketing Plan is commonly referred to as "the Plan." Read it cover to cover. Have it explained to you.

- Go to a meeting or two to see how people are trained.

- Listen to a few tapes. Ask for audiotapes about people's experiences in this business. Ask for, and listen to, training tapes. These will be the tools that you will have to learn from.

- Read a book or two from the book list (pp. 119-120).

- Ask questions and get answers. Take the time to absorb and understand the information. Like anything new, there are many details to learn about. If you don't understand something, ask.

- Review the items that your prospective sponsor gave you. Look through the catalogs. Find items that interest you.

- Try the products. The person who showed you the plan should have left some with you. If not, then ask for some.
- See how products flow to the consumer. Place an order for some products that you can personally use. Follow the process from the placement of the order with the person who has shown you the plan, to the processing of the order, to the pick-up from the Direct Distributor or the delivery from Amway to the person with whom you placed your order, and finally to you.

and, most importantly,

- Check out the people. John Sestina said, "I'd rather be in a bad deal with good people than in a good deal with bad people." Get around the people who are succeeding in the business, and do your homework. Meet the people who are upline from the person who has shown you the plan. Meet their upline including their Direct Distributor and, if possible, their upline Diamond. Ask yourself: Could I form a mentoring relationship with at least two of the people in this line of sponsorship (upline)? In this business, you really need to learn from those people who are your upline.

HOW TO GET STARTED IN THIS BUSINESS

Recommended books:

Compassionate Capitalism **by** Rich DeVos
Rich DeVos, cofounder of Amway, offers a proven plan that helped him become one of the richest men in America. Sharing his amazing story, and the stories of men and women from around the world, DeVos shows how success is achieved and what it truly means.

Promises to Keep **by** Charles Paul Conn
A detailed perspective on the truly pioneering phenomenon of the Amway Corporation, the number one Network Marketing company in the world.

Future Choice **by** Michael S. Clouse and Kathie Jackson Anderson
A discussion of why Network Marketing may be your best career move.

Network Marketing Window of Opportunity **by** Jeffrey Babener
A renowned lawyer in the field of Network Marketing describes Network Marketing in terms that are clear and concise. (Don't be fooled by the small size of this book—34 pages.)

NETWORK MARKETING: THE BEST OF THE BEST

Other recommended books:

The Possible Dream by Charles Paul Conn

An Uncommon Freedom by Charles Paul Conn

How to Be Rich by J. Paul Getty

How to Win Friends and Influence People by Dale Carnegie

Marketing Warfare by Al Ries and Jack Trout

The 22 Immutable Laws of Marketing by Al Ries and Jack Trout

The Magic of Thinking Big by David J. Schwartz

Think and Grow Rich by Napoleon Hill

Wave 3: New Era in Network Marketing by Richard Poe

How Secure Is Your Financial Future? by Allen Baytes

Should You Quit Before You're Fired? by Paul Zane Pilzer

Network Marketing Action Guide for Success by David Stewart

The Network Marketer's Guide to Success by Jeffrey Babener and David Stewart

The Popcorn Report by Faith Popcorn

Winner's Circle by Charles Paul Conn

Believe by Charles Paul Conn and Rich DeVos

HOW TO GET STARTED IN THIS BUSINESS

These books are only the "tip of the iceberg." There are many books you can read that will help you in this business. Ask the person who showed you the plan to share his or her book list with you. Read a book or two from the list. Also listen to a few of the audiotapes that this person recommends.

Recommended audiotapes:

Escape the Rat Race

The Blinding Paradigm

A Financial Planner's Viewpoint

The Concept of the People's Franchise

Network Marketing, The Business Vehicle of the 90s

There are several steps that you should take once you are ready to make the commitment to get into this business.

Some strategies for success

Reassure yourself

To reassure yourself that you have chosen the right company and to get a feel for the dynamism that captures the spirit of Amway, ask your sponsor to introduce you to some other people who are currently in the business. Talk with them and get their thoughts and ideas on Amway. If you find out for yourself from people who are actually in the business rather than simply hearing it through tapes or reading it from books, you will go into it knowing that you are honestly making the right decision for yourself and you will feel much more at ease having done so. Tapes and literature are great materials for teaching you all about the business, its philosophy, and roadways to success, but there is nothing like actually talking to your future upline people and seeing how your own ideals and philosophies coincide with theirs. Amway is a people business. The people that you will be working with are very important. This support system is unique to Amway and is one of the critical aspects to its having such a high success rate among its independent distributors.

HOW TO GET STARTED IN THIS BUSINESS

Check out the products again

Once you are convinced of the uniqueness of the Amway program and the tremendous opportunities available to those who seek and pursue them, the next important step is to check over the products again. There must be no doubt in your mind. The products must be of such high quality that you would be willing to buy them for yourself and your family even if no marketing plan ever existed from the company. You must believe in them. In Amway's case, the products are of the highest quality found anywhere in the world. Again—you must make up your own mind on this and not just take the word of tapes or friends. Try them out. Compare them to the other products you are currently using. When you are convinced from your own research that Amway products are the best, then you will be working with a company you really do believe in, and you can start talking to people about the products and company without having to make excuses for anything less than the best.

Check out the company

If you believe in the philosophy and the ideals of the company, and you believe in the products, then you will also believe in yourself. One of the most difficult tasks in life is to have to work for a company or an organization whose products you do not believe in or whose beliefs you do not share. Your energy level is never very high, and your frustration level is always seething below the surface. One of the reasons for Amway's tremendous success is the belief held by the vast majority of its employees and independent distributors that they are working in flow with their ideals and moral convictions rather than against them. This uniformly-held belief system is responsible, in our opinion, for much of the energy you will discover when you meet with other independent distributors and attend meetings.

Enroll as an independent distributor
The actual enrollment process simply involves the purchase of a business (sales and products) kit from your sponsor and the filling out of an Amway Distributor Application. This kit contains several Amway products, an Amway Business Reference Manual, the Amway Sales and Marketing Plan, several sales catalogs, an assortment of business forms and sales information (to help you get started), and a welcome video cassette. The application includes your name, address, phone number, social security number, and the names of those in your upline—from your sponsor to your upline Direct Distributor. It also includes a one-page contract that defines your relationship to Amway and authorizes you to act as an Amway distributor. Amway assigns you an Amway Distributor Association (A.D.A.) number, which is used to track your personal and group sales volume. You are never required to purchase or maintain product

HOW TO GET STARTED IN THIS BUSINESS

inventory. The rest is up to you. Speak with your sponsor and let him or her show you how to get "plugged into" the legendary Amway success path. If your goal is to succeed "big time," you will be amazed at how quickly your upline people will do everything in their power to offer you their support, knowledge, and time to carry you toward the fulfillment of your dreams.

This may sound unbelievable to those who are unfamiliar with how Amway works, but it is, in reality, the way the program is intended to work. It was set up to allow the individual the opportunity to become "plugged into" a system that almost assures success for the person who really wants to achieve that success. This is one of the major reasons we are so impressed with Amway. As far as we know, there are no other Network Marketing companies that offer this tremendous educational advantage and proven method for achievement.

Learn from your sponsor and upline

When you enroll into Amway, be willing to work with your sponsor and your upline and learn from them how to support and build your own downline. Be willing to learn from their experiences. Do not be close-minded. Study their successes. Mentor their actions. Keep an open mind and you will be surprised at the results.

Support your downline

Learn to disregard the notion that your goals come first and those of the people in your organization come second. This "me first" philosophy will not work well in Network Marketing. Amway has understood this concept from the beginning and has incorporated it into a cornerstone of its organizational strategy. As an independent distributor, you should always put the dreams and goals of your downline before your own. Once they begin to realize the attainment of their own dreams, usually of financial success and personal freedom, their prosperity will come back to you in multiples that you never dreamed possible. Your organization is only as strong as the people in it, and their success and attainment of goals will only assure yours.

Rich DeVos and Jay Van Andel, founders of Amway, did not become two of the wealthiest men in America by stepping on people or treating them unfairly, nor did they build one of the mightiest and most dynamic organizations in the world by initiating policies of inequality, subordination, or greed. Rather, they did exactly the opposite (read *Compassionate Capitalism* by Rich DeVos). They created an environment within the organization that allowed the "creative juices" of all of their employees and independent distributors to freely flow. They created an atmosphere of trust and support that, to this day, is a pillar of their organization. They created an environment that allowed for all of their independent distributors to follow their dreams. Those who stuck to it and accepted the help and advice that Amway had to offer often became very wealthy as a result.

Rich DeVos and Jay Van Andel set up a program that allowed others to become wealthy because they knew that in allowing others to succeed they in turn would be justly rewarded. This philosophy creates a power in Amway that we have not seen in any other Network Marketing company. It can foster a power in your own organization that can create the force to assure your own success.

This is a powerful strategy, but one which is in fact mostly ignored by most other Network Marketing organizations, where the philosophy is often to get as much as you can out of the company in quick profits and to use your downline to achieve your own short-term objectives. Amway's philosophy is exactly the opposite and teaches that by building up and helping your downline, you in turn will reap the long-term benefits.

If you actually study the lives of the majority of Network Marketing millionaires and attempt to find a common thread that links them all together, it is probably the care, the support, and the confidence-building they impart to their downlines that bind them all together. Granted, they are all highly motivated, but that is about where the similarities end. They come from all types of backgrounds, different countries and cultures, and differing levels of education and abilities. But they nearly all take a personal interest in their downline people. Even after retirement, when they are just sitting at home or abroad collecting their residual income, they often stay in touch with their downline people, even though they certainly do not have to. They tend to be people who, for the moment, put their own dreams aside to help fulfill the dreams of other people. They realize that their downlines consist of people, not PIN numbers and social security numbers. They impart this philosophy to the people in their downlines, making their organizations very dynamic and energized. As you multiply this enthusiasm by the many thousands of downlines that exist in Amway, you can envision the energy and dynamism that will propel the company into the next century—and far beyond.

One final note—
This business takes a lot of time and effort to become successful. In fact, almost anything worth accomplishing requires a significant effort. If becoming a millionaire were easy and could be achieved by simply joining a Network Marketing company, then we would all be millionaires. When you join this business, you become part of a team of people who reach their goals and dreams by helping others.

Do not let your experiences in the Corporate World strip you of your hope and dreams. Instead, learn from those experiences, and search out a means to achieve your dreams. This business offers a means of achieving financial freedom and the time to enjoy having it. With financial freedom, you can dream again.

A dream brings the hope of a better future into life. Financial freedom and the time to enjoy having it are just the beginning....

Rich DeVos says it best, "Dreaming is the first step of a lifelong trek away from mediocrity and failure, toward accomplishment and a sense of fulfillment and self-worth."[1]

He goes on to say, "Don't set goals that are too small or too safe. Dare to dream big dreams that are far beyond where you are. Anyone can set a goal safely to walk across the street. Take a giant step. See the world. Why settle for mediocre goals when you can achieve something really wonderful? Believe in yourself! Follow your dream! Those are the really big steps. Everything else will follow."[2]

What is your dream?

---

[1]. Rich DeVos, *Compassionate Capitalism*, Plume (Penguin Books), 1994, p. 47.

[2]. Ibid., p. 212.